Coventry Memories

The publishers would like to thank the following companies for their

support in the production of this book

Main Sponsor
Jaguar Cars

Amtico Company

Bablake School

Bablake Wines Limited

KB Benfield Holdings Limited

Bennetts Insurance Specialists

Coventry Building Society

Cov Con

Dunlop Aviation

Ellisons

Flanagan & Sons

W Grace Removals

Grimmett & Timms

Norman Hay Plc

Marconi Communications

Power Torque Engineering

Sofedit UK Limited

First published in Great Britain by True North Books Limited
England HX3 6AE
01422 344344

ISBN 1 903204 69 0

Text, design and origination by True North Books Limited
Printed and bound in Great Britain

Coventry Memories

Contents

Introduction

Time acts as a filter and removes from our memories all the things that we thought to be bad when we were experiencing them. Or it changes our perception of them so that they can be joked about fondly. Ration books and gas masks that featured so strongly in the lives of those who remember them suddenly become lost, eccentric old friends. Thank goodness that the past is looked at through rose-coloured spectacles. Everyone's history becomes 'the good old days'. We argue that technology may be improving some aspects of life today, but 'there aren't the same values today'. 'People get things too easily, and don't have the same sense of appreciation', 'and people were better mannered and courteous to one another'. Whether there is any truth in these statements or not, they are an important part of our personal histories, and helped to shape our characters. We think things were better then. 'You could go shopping in town and leave your front door unlocked'. Now that these times have gone their passing is regretted. Cars, and even bicycles, seen in these old pictures are reminders of a faithful 'old girl', who was, regretfully, sent to the scrap yard. ' would they have been worth today?' 'I wish that I still had my old Austin Seven'. Immediately we forget the difficulty starting the engine on a cold day. The number of times we had to push it down the road, jumping in at the last moment. We quickly put it into gear and bumped the clutch to turn the engine in the hopes that it would fire into life before the bottom of the hill was reached. There was no heater and few other creature comforts, but it had character and personality, and so we gave it a name to suit.

Butcher Row in 1936 prior to the demolition gangs moving in.

Continued from previous page: More often than not, it would be a girl's name, like 'Genevieve', or 'Lucy'. Presented with photographs of familiar places, the spark ignites the memories and they flash through our minds again as freshly as if yesterday. This book is the blue touchpaper of nostalgia. Even the buildings and streets, which at the time were considered unimportant, are now cherished friends whose passing is mourned.

In Coventry, this sense of belonging to place, and the pain of loss, was etched into the hearts and minds of the people in a way that could not happen in many other places. A new word entered our vocabulary in 1940. That word was 'Blitz'. In one single night much of their familiar landscape was changed forever. Even these terrible memories slowly take on values that make us believe that the experiences were, somehow,

Crowds of excited people await the arrival of King George VI and Queen Elizabeth in April 1951.

character building. Perhaps they were, because they made the people more determined to "rise from the ashes", as symbolised by the Phoenix carved on the levelling stone. Coventry is a magical place of towers, spires, and Lady Godiva, and tremendous optimism. It is not surprising that the enemy saw Coventry as a major threat and, therefore a major target. Whitley and Lancaster bombers were being produced at the Armstrong Whitworth plant at Whitley. Rootes Group were producing both bombers and military vehicles of all kinds. Standard made Gypsy Moths and Mosquitoes fighter planes. Jaguar were making both bomber and fighter plane parts as well as military vehicles. Daimler alone made 50,000 aero-engines. They also built armoured and scout cars. Alvis produced armoured vehicles and tanks. Talk about the war effort!

Around the city centre

Take a cobbled surface, polish it with the metal wheels of the occasional horse and cart, add a thin film of rubber and oil from the cars, wet it with a shower of rain, mix in a hundred cyclists on their way home from work, pepper it with a few day dreaming pedestrians with no road sense whatsoever, and you have a disaster waiting to happen. One policeman's helmet has turned white with the shock of having to sort out this traffic problem. His sergeant seems equally bemused. He is not in favour of erecting a statue to commemorate James Starley, the inventor of the bicycle, in Warwick Row, or anywhere else for that matter. He is wishing that the cycle industry had been founded in China. At least these are the 'safety' bicycles invented by his nephew John Kemp Starley, and not the penny-farthings that James, along with William Hillman, patented. Though nobody looks very safe with all these bikes dashing about. Won't the police be glad when the 50s arrive and they are lifted from harms way into one of those striped boxes? Or better still give Coventry some of those robotic traffic lights, which were first installed outside the House of Commons in 1914. Why can't someone write a little book giving drivers, cyclists, motorcyclists and pedestrians a few rules of the road? We could call it the 'Highway Code'. Sorry you will have to wait until 1931 for that to happen!

Although passers-by appear to show little interest in the timbered buildings in Spon Street, there was growing concern that many timber-framed buildings of such historic significance had been lost, as much through redevelopment as from destruction during the bombing raids on Coventry in 1940 and 1941. By 1963, when this picture was taken, plans were being considered for the preservation of the best of the remaining buildings. Many were dismantled from other parts of the city and reconstructed in Spon Street. Our picture shows numbers 159 to 162 Spon Street. Numbers 157 to 158 were sacrificed for the construction of the inner ring road.

'Coventry's leading record stockist' would, no doubt, be playing the music of those boys from Liverpool with the funny haircuts and Italian styled suits, on the 'Audio Sound', equipment. Stereophonic records, played on machines in teak cabinets with twin speakers, produced a more realistic sound than ever before. The Beatles burst onto the music scene. They had eleven consecutive number one hits between 1963 and 1966. The Rolling Stones with the 'rubber lipped' Mick Jagger as lead singer were formed in 1963. Many still favoured their radios and would sit alongside the Bakelite brown curved box to listen to their favourite programmes and listen to the newest records.

Below: Pedestrians wander where they will in the centre of Broadgate. The trams clang and rumble along the road, their tracks dominating the centre, they are unable to take avoiding action. All others must move to make way. Their metal wheels polish the surface of the tracks to gleam like mirrors. When, in 1940, the bombers roared overhead carrying their deadly cargo of bombs, the canals, rivers, and these well shone tram lines reflected the bright moon of the night. It clearly marked the city target. The National Provincial Bank was one of the few buildings to miraculously remain standing in this area after the war. The streets have been widened and traffic moves smoothly. Cars in 1939, when this camera's shutter snapped, seemed to have more individuality than their modern relatives. Car spotting can become a fascinating game with the resulting picture. Parked on the left beyond Whitfield's there is a little three-wheeler with a boat tailed back. Many lightweight cars were built with this particular configuration. The Coventry Victor three-wheeler was advertised as being 'Vibrationless'. On these cobbled roads it is difficult to imagine any vehicle, other than the tram, to be 'vibrationless'.

The sight of army lorries would soon become a familiar sight. Preparations were being made for war, which many now accepted as inevitable. The Home Office delivered thousands of air-raid shelters, which had been developed under the watchful eye of Sir John Anderson, to homes in London. These 'Anderson shelters' soon occupied the gardens of homes in Coventry as well as those in London.

Below right: In the 50s and 60s there was rebellion. The generation gap was created when the adolescents of the fifties had their own opinions about dress and music, and a great deal more. They swung their hoola-hoops around their waists in a provocative manner, and the word 'teenager' was coined to describe this group that did not fit comfortably into the categories of child or adult. With hair swept back into a 'DA', they wore their 'teddy' suits in the Edwardian style. With crepe soled shoes, velvet collars and tight drainpipe trousers they swept into the dance halls like the Orchard Ballroom in Primrose Hill Street. They 'bopped' to the rock and roll songs. What girl could resist such peacocks? Unless, of course, the girls preferred the 'Mod' style, with the Italian 'winkle-picker' shoes, well polished and pointed. What a sense of style they had. How many can remember the 'Cha-Cha' dance, imported from Cuba in 1955? In those days it was fashionable and 'macho' to smoke, even sporting heroes did it. Lovers on the cinema screen smoked after the sea had finished crashing against the shore, and the music had faded. Tobacco was laid inside a machine for 'rolling your own'. The paper was fed into the last fraction of an inch and then gently wetted with the tongue. The machine wrapped the paper around the tobacco to make a thin cigarette, never firm and even like the one on the poster. The first third of the creation vanished with the first light, from a petrol lighter. Remember those little rubber 'torpedoes' full of petrol? We nipped off the end and carefully squeezed the petrol onto the cotton wool that packed the inside of the lighter.

Bottom: The number 21 is ready for the journey back to the city. In the years after the war public transport was still the way for most people to get about. The trams ceased to function after bombing had torn up most of their tracks, the rest were removed as they had always been a hazard for the wheels of other road users. In many places the cobbled base remained for a while, later to be covered with a layer of tarmacadam. The overhead cables, which delivered the power to the tram's pantograph (that arm which attached itself to the cable) also vanished from the landscape. The pantographs showered sparks on icy days as the trams glided smoothly along the road. If the driver could have heard the words of those sitting in the living rooms of the houses that he passed, he would have been surprised at the strength of the language. As the occupants sat, squinting at the small purple television screen, the interference from the electric arm of the tram crackled across the surface of the screen in noisy wavy patterns. Many cars, and worst of all motorcycles, produced the same effect if a suppressor did not cover their spark plugs. It was difficult enough to keep the picture on the screen from rolling by carefully adjusting the vertical and horizontal hold controls, without further problems.

At the junction of Old Church Road and Bell Green, an old lamp sits opposite a younger, more modern, and considerably taller, concrete relative. It is easy to picture George Formby leaning on the old lamppost and waiting for a "certain little lady" to pass by, but the other seems to lack the romance somehow.

Above: Don't ever say that there is never a policeman when you want one. Here he waits, on the corner of Hales Street and Burges, in the years between the wars, ready to direct traffic, and not a vehicle in sight. Not even one of Coventry's famous bicycles. It is a bumpy ride for any vehicle on the cobbles and over the tramlines with only coach springs for suspension. Even cars could find life difficult if their wheels slipped into the iron tramlines. For bicycles or motorcycles, it could be most dangerous. The art was to cross them as close to right angles as possible to avoid them taking over the steering and throwing the rider. Pennington Autocars boasted in their adverts for the machine that, 'it can run over tramlines at any angle with perfect safety'. The cobblestones developed a smooth, polished surface from the metal-rimmed cartwheels. Buffed up with a coat of rubber from tyres, and wet with rain, it made a lethal combination. Should there have been an accident on this spot from the twelfth to the fourteenth century, the Hospital of St John the Baptist could deal with the casualties. Later a 'Free Grammar School' was established in the premises, which eventually moved to Warwick Road and became King Henry VIII School. All that has survived is a fourteenth century church, which replaced the original chapel.
W H Croft's have a display of poultry and fish, which would have given the modern Health and Safety Officer a heart attack.

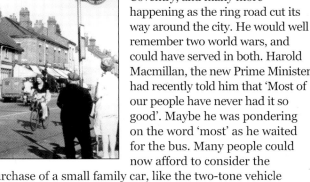

At least if a food inspector were to telephone he would only have to remember a three-figure number.

Below centre: The elderly gentleman at the bus stop may well be bringing the lady's attention to the Medieval trenched roof trusses, collar beam and queen struts on the gable end of A C Buckle's old premises in Spon Street. Or he may be commenting on the wonders of television as the aerials begin to sprout from every roof in the late 50s. In his lifetime he must have witnessed many changes in Coventry, and many more happening as the ring road cut its way around the city. He would well remember two world wars, and could have served in both. Harold Macmillan, the new Prime Minister had recently told him that 'Most of our people have never had it so good'. Maybe he was pondering on the word 'most' as he waited for the bus. Many people could now afford to consider the purchase of a small family car, like the two-tone vehicle parked at the opposite sided of the road.
If it is Saturday teatime as the camera shutter snapped, the lady on the bicycle could be dashing home to catch the 'Six Five Special coming down the line'. It was an extremely popular programme introducing new British stars, like Tommy Steel who sang about his 'Little White Bull'. Maybe he could compete with the American star, Elvis Presley?'

Below centre: As we look up Trinity Street from Swanswell Gate in the 50s, little seems to have changed, except it seems that it was much easier to cross the road. Perhaps the secret of crossing safely rested in the fact that you started with a Double Diamond? Drink one, was the message of the posters of the time, and you could achieve anything. They 'Worked Wonders' was the promise they made. Drink two and who knows the result? Crossings had received their stripes in 1951 and their beacons flashed a warning to drivers in 1952. The cars were driven more slowly in those days and required the driver to anticipate the actions of others well in advance. The car in front probably had no stoplights or flashing indicators, as these were only made compulsory in 1965. The mechanical 'traficators', the arms with a light bulb inside an orange plastic cover, did not always lift out of their housings as reliably as one would have liked. Many a driver had to bang the doorpost with his fist to release the sticking arm, or quickly wind down the window and give a hand-signal.

Below: Like removing your hand from a bucket of water and looking for the hole it has left - The stalls of West Orchard fish market, like all the other shops and businesses in Coventry which were destroyed by the bombing, were quickly erected and back in business almost in the blink of an eye. Behind them the scaffolding goes up and the city rises and recovers beneath the shadows of the surviving spires.

Quiet on this morning in the fifties, but usually thronging with keen shoppers looking for some fresh fish for the table. There is even time for the stallholder to exchange a witty remark or two to the men passing on their way to work. They are not about to break the four-minute mile in the way that the 25-year-old medical student, Roger Bannister, did in 1954. He was the first man ever to break the four-minute barrier. He attributed it to his new scientifically based training techniques.

The weather is fine at the moment, but in cinemas throughout the land, Gene Kelly is splashing through puddles and 'Singin' in the Rain'. London is suffering the worst 'Peasoupers' it has ever experienced. That lethal mixture of black, sooty smoke, and fog, stirred into a deadly cocktail with the fumes of traffic. Anti-smog masks were distributed, but over two thousand people died from heart and lung diseases as a direct result of it. The Clean Air Act was urgently needed.

Has anyone thought of creating a board game for the people of Coventry? Using a plan of the city as it was here, shortly after Princess Elizabeth laid the foundation stone for the redevelopment of Broadgate in 1948, the object of the game would be to mark as many changes that have taken place over the years since. Using the few remaining landmarks as a guide, later buildings and roads must be placed as accurately as possible. The spires would help, as would the National Provincial Bank seen to the right of the Island. Players in the game could have the task of spotting landmarks, which still exist, and those that were sacrificed for the development of the city centre, or those that were scooped away as the ring road carved its way across the landscape. Two points could be given for spotting St Mary's Guildhall, and two more for the Council House. More points could be earned for knowing that Lady Godiva's statue arrived in the centre of the green in 1949. Earl Street leading to Gosford Street and out towards Stoke may give further clues in this difficult game. Finding the Scala Cinema in Gosford Street, later called the Odeon, may prove more difficult. It had the distinction of being the first in Coventry to show 'talkies'. It seems incredible that the first words spoken on the talking films were not poetic words conveying a deep message to commemorate that historic moment, but Al Jolson blurting out, 'Wait a minute! Wait a minute! You ain't heard nuthin' yet.' 'D'you wanna hear 'Toot-toot-tootsie'?' During the war the cinemas gave much needed escapism from the austere life outside. Whilst the ladies made the best of their old clothes they could at least admire the silk and velvet dresses with plunging necklines in films such as 'The Wicked Lady'. They pictured themselves in the place of Margaret Lockwood and forgot their ration books for the moment.

Memorable moments

I t is difficult to understand the reasons why so many of the citizens of the town are gathered here, in Broadgate, on 12 December 1936, to listen to the announcement that Edward VIII was abdicating. Prince Albert, they were told, would take the crown and wished to be known as George VI. It seems incredible too that the national newspapers had agreed to keep a code of silence around the story of Edward and Mrs Wallis Simpson. Foreign reporters did not feel the same obligation and had published the story, so it was fairly common knowledge anyway. The church of the time denounced divorce, and, since the King was Head of the Church of England, the idea of him marrying a divorcee was improper. Marriage was for life. Men were the breadwinners and the women had a duty to remain in the home. Only war changed attitudes towards women at work. The family consisted of a man, his married wife, and their children. Any woman or man deviating from this accepted pattern was immediately shunned. Curtains would move as they passed down the street, and tongues would wag. With such narrow attitudes so strongly entrenched the situation was unacceptable to many, although it was also mixed with a little sympathy for their plight, as well as a little admiration for Edward's sacrifice for his love. As the people assembled here, a destroyer of the Royal Navy, HMS Fury, slipped away from Portsmouth harbour carrying the ex-king to, what was reported in the following day's papers as 'an unknown destination'. Four short years after the camera recorded this scene, all of the shops in the street were destroyed.

The Union Jacks are out, and so are the bargains at the clothiers, as the Duke of York rides by on Tuesday 10 December 1935. The Midland Bank customers and workers have thronged the pavement or left their work to gaze from the windows in the hope of getting a glimpse of the Duke. He was on his way, with the mayor, Alderman Charles Payne, to open the new Technical College. In his speech he commented that it was 'very cheering' to be in Coventry 'in the midst of manufacturing activity and development'. He praised the citizens and public-spirited men of Coventry for having recognised the need to train highly skilled men 'to meet the demand placed upon them in this modern age of machinery'. No one could know, at this time, that their future king was addressing them. Events moved swiftly. George V died a month after this visit, on 20 January 1936, and Edward VIII succeeded him. Edward wished to marry Mrs Wallis Simpson, an American divorcee. The king was advised not to marry her as the people of the country, and the Commonwealth, would not accept her as queen. Edward proposed that he would be king, but that she would not be called queen, nor would any children of the marriage be in line for the throne. This compromise was not accepted. The monarch is head of the church, which at the time was strongly opposed to divorce. The British newspapers agreed a code of silence over the affair. A thing that seems incredible today. The foreign press, however, gave no such undertaking. The king abdicated.

There were many road schemes needed to open the city centre for modern transport. Roads such as Butcher Row (*bottom*) and Little Butcher Row (*centre*) were fine for the horse drawn carts of the past, but this was the era of the motorcar. Such narrow streets could not accommodate trams buses and cars. In January 1936, defined as a 'slum', Butcher Row was to be cleared in the name of progress. There were great reductions to be had at Jacob's, in the previous weeks. Lots of 'closing down bargains' had been available throughout Butcher Row. Maybe some of the hats and caps worn on this occasion were purchased there. The Mayor, Alderman Charles Payne, with due ceremony and a long speech, closed the roads for demolition work to begin. Out with the old and in with the new. Shops and stalls selling fish, meat, and furniture amongst other things flanked the narrow, cobbled, Butcher Row. Beneath the flickering naphtha flares of the street lamps vendors cried out their bargains. This Dickensian scene would have been loved by the tourists of today. Valued now, and reconstructed with loving care in Spon Street, the half-timbered buildings were of little value and unappreciated at this time. Final sales were over and the premises vacated. Sadly there was no thought for the preservation of architecturally interesting buildings. There was no attempt to preserve slices of history and amalgamate them with the new and so many Victorian buildings of note vanished. But we should not be too critical. How many modern, or indeed 50s buildings do we look upon now as having great beauty and aesthetic value? There was no Spon Street plan in 1936. This was progress and a move from the depression of earlier years into a bright future, which was ensured by the growing car industry. Trinity Street would open in 1937 providing a wide carriageway through which such cars could pass. It is only with the wisdom of hindsight that we see old properties as having historic value. How many, and which, of our modern buildings will achieve this status of being architecturally and historically valuable records of our time? Traffic was increasing and it was economically sensible to create better access for materials to be moved in and out of the city. Motorists were receiving splendid value for money when they bought cars like the new 14hp Wolseley. Two hundred pounds for the saloon and thirty-five pounds more for the de-luxe model, which had dual arm windscreen wipers, triplex glass in all windows, chromium plated headlamps, bumpers and louvred vents on the bonnet.

Although the sun was shining, there was enough breeze blowing to move the length of Coventry tape, but not sufficient to remove hats from heads. Though some had removed them to save them from being blown into the crowd. A person's hat clearly indicated his or her social status, as surely as the crown of England. The Mayor, as he cut the ribbon to officially open Trinity Street in 1937, wore the well-brushed top hat. His lady has as many flowers on hers as in the bouquet she is holding. Professional gentlemen and officials sport bowlers or the ever-popular homburgs, whilst the flat caps and headscarves are not only at the back of the crowd, but also well down the social ladder. Thanks to the Queen the headscarf became acceptable for all ranks.

The sun seemed to be shining on the whole of Britain in 1937, but in Europe the war clouds were gathering.

Many people had a little more money in their pockets than they had had in the previous decade. The new twelve-sided three-penny bit came into circulation. It rested in your purse along with the silver 'tanner' (sixpence), and that other pretty little coin bearing a picture of a wren, the farthing (one quarter of a penny), and the ha'penny (half-penny) with its galleon under full sail. Coins in those days had an eccentric charm. The crown, worth five shillings (twenty-five new pence) was falling into disuse, but the half-crown, a generous sized coin with weight and wealth worth two shillings and six pence (twelve and a half new pence) was still going strong. Retrospectively they may seem illogical, but didn't we fight to try to keep them, and wasn't their passing mourned? Not to mention the ten-shilling note, and the pound note.

Princess Elizabeth cut the silk ribbon with a pair of gold scissors at the inauguration of the new city centre in May 1948 (*centre*). The ribbon was, of course, the finest silk ribbon made in Coventry as it has been since the seventeenth century. It was decorated with a motif inspired by the new plan of Broadgate, on a sky-blue ground in red, green, and royal blue. It had a narrow border of red on one edge and green on the other. It also had the words 'Her Royal Highness Princess Elizabeth', and 'Broadgate, Coventry, 22 May 1948'. The princess was fashionably dressed in an outfit which was predominately lime-green with up to the minute open back and open toe shoes with an ankle strap. The newspapers reported that she was wearing some make-up, but in tasteful moderation. In the 40s and early 50s it was still considered a little vulgar and risky to use make-up. After the austere war years ladies were becoming increasingly fashion conscious. Rationing was not yet at an end, and even when the measures were lifted, the goods were not always available in the shops. Even three years later, in 1951, the government had to regulate prices in order to give a fair deal to all. The Evening Telegraph reported the case of two brothers, from Foleshill Road, who had been fined for selling nylon stockings at eight shillings and eleven pence

(about 45 new pence), which was 16 new pence above the controlled price of five shillings and nine pence. They were fined ten pounds each with two guineas costs (a guinea being one pound and one shilling - or 105 new pence). They deserved this stiff fine.

It was a hot sunny day in May 1948 as the crowds gathered around the temporary stand from which Princess Elizabeth would perform the ceremony of laying the foundation stone of a new shopping precinct in Broadgate (*below*). It was to be the first of its kind in Britain. Many had waited several hours for the arrival of the Royal visitor. No doubt the services of the nurses, seen at the edge of the crowd would be needed. Smelling salts would be wafted under the noses of several who fainted in the heat of the sun. At a little after three in the afternoon there was an almighty cheer as the Princess arrived escorted by the mayor and with a guard of honour provided by HMS Gamecock, the Royal Navy Air Training School, at Bramcote. Few could have guessed that the Princess, who was married to the Duke of Edinburgh the previous year, would give birth to her first child, Prince Charles, before the end of the year. Nor could they have realised that in four short and busy years she would become Queen.

With tassels and flags at the ready they wait on the edge of the pavement for the arrival of King George and Queen Elizabeth. The weather is fine, but there is a chill in the air on this April day in 1951. Most, as was the fashion, are sensibly wearing some form of hat, whether it is a bonnet knitted by mother, a felt hat, or a headscarf. The school cap is no longer popular, but it always gave the smart finishing touches to our school uniform. Without it the girls would have nothing to snatch and run away with, knowing for certain that the boy was chasing them. It was an essential part of the ritual of letting them know that there was an attraction. The boys returned the expression of their blossoming love with a pull on her plaits. The gentleman, if he had read the day's newspaper, would have received the devastating news from the American Academy of Science, who announced in 1951, that there is definitely no cure for baldness!

When the thrill of witnessing the royal visit is over they may all return home to press their ears to the radio to listen to the new story of a family; 'The Archers' - 'a tale of everyday folk' has just begun this year. The children may want the popular, if rather crazy, comedy, which features some very strange characters, called 'The Goons'. 'With such a name it surely cannot last. It is probably a passing fad. Give it a month or two and it will be forgotten', many a dad would say.

Right: With the Mayor of Coventry, Alderman Howat, leading the way, the King and Queen move from Broadgate House, where they had just made a 'balcony appearance' to the joy of the crowd on this glorious sunny day in April 1951. Everyone commented on the unrestrained way in which the royal couple put people at their ease. However, despite the smiles and disarming manner, the King was showing signs that his illness was beginning to get the better of him. Many in the crowd would not be aware of just how ill he was, unless they observed him carefully. His face was pale and drawn. He was terminally ill from cancer. In May he and the Queen opened the Festival of Britain Exhibition, and in June it was planned that he should go on a six-month tour of the commonwealth. The King was concerned about the difficulties faced by the Prime Minister Attlee, who had also been ill, and knew that a general election was imminent. Princess Elizabeth and Prince Phillip took the King's place on the tour of the Commonwealth, and, in September while they were away, the King underwent an operation. In the operating theatre in Buckingham Palace, his left lung was removed as the cancer had advanced. In February 1952, whilst he was at Sandringham, he died.

Below: The King and Queen Elizabeth walk through the ruined cathedral during their visit on 5 April 1951. They had been met at the south door and the Mayor had presented the Bishop of Coventry, Dr. Neville Gorton and Mrs. Gorton. As they moved through the ruins they paused for a moment to see the Chapel of Resurrection and the Chapel of Unity. They had previously visited in 1942 to see the plans for the redevelopment of the city after the blitz, and, at that time they were only plans. The following month the King and Queen opened the Festival of Britain. It was to be the kick-start to industries, which provided a shop window to the world to show that Britain was 'back in business'. It was an opportunity for everyone to give themselves a much deserved 'pat on the back' as they moved along the road to recovery. It transformed the 27 acre bombsite on the South Bank of the Thames into a village containing pavilions, sculptures, and a Festival Hall. Children throughout the land could imagine the wonders of it, as paper cutout models allowed them to build their own Festival. The cigar shaped 'Skylon', and the centrepiece of the exhibition, the 'Dome of Discovery', were glimpses of what the future may now hold for Britain. The Festival of Britain was organised by Labour Minister Herbert Morrison. It may not be coincidence that the concept of a dome might be used by his grandson, Peter Mandelson, as inspiration for a Millennium Dome at Greenwich.

Lady Godiva once rode her horse (on the statue of course) in the middle of Garden Island in Broadgate, but she had to take it a little closer to the precinct in more recent times, to make way for the construction of Cathedral Lanes Shopping Centre. Behind the Drummers we can see the Tudor style shops and Owen Owen, at the top of Trinity Street on this calm sunny day in 1951.

The Queen has a question to ask the mayor, as he leans forward attentively. This 'unrestrained manner' which she and the King had, was reported in the newspapers as 'making everyone - from civic leaders to the humblest family feel at home'. She could be enquiring to see if he had remembered to apply for his ration book. The method of doing so had been clearly laid out in the newspapers during the month of April. Rationing still continued, and such matters were important, as customers had to register with a retailer. Life was still difficult for a long time after hostilities were ended. The lady in the fashionable fur wrap was not at risk of being pelted with missiles as she may have been today, but wore it proudly as a sign that coupons, to her at least, did not limit her when she purchased her wardrobe, or it may well be that she, like all the ladies of the time, had learnt the lessons of 'make do and mend'. Old clothes were made to look like new with a little careful tuck here and a stitch there. Nothing was wasted and much ingenuity was shown.

Below: These are the days that remain in the minds of children, and adults, for the rest of their lives. As we think back over our lives, it is the school pantomime when the teacher played the fairy-godmother, or the presentation day (speech day as they were also called) when we received our book prize, a school trip, or the day we welcomed Princess Margaret to Coventry, that are the mileposts of our memories.

As she stepped from the car at the Cathedral, the Bishop, Dr Cuthbert Bardsley, greeted her, and led the way into the ruined Cathedral. Following close behind was the Mayor

Mrs Alderman P M Hyde, looking quite splendid in her formal robes. Hay Lane was lined with men from the RAF, and a flag waving, cheering, crowd. A peal of bells rang out a welcome. It was reported in the newspaper that she showed great interest in a display of photographs showing the cathedral before and after the bombing.

The freedom to print the news, and the protection of an individual's privacy, has always been a sensitive balance for the press. Until the 70s the private lives of the royal family were generally left alone, but Princess Margaret featured highly in the gossip columns two years prior to her visit to

Coventry in 1957. Her romance with Group Captain Peter Townsend, a divorcee, got the tongues wagging. Later, when she encountered pressure from the church and the government, it was called off. That provided further material for the gossip columns of the newspapers. People were reminded of the abdication of her uncle and the controversy that followed.

Bottom right: A young, 21 year old, Princess Alexandra presided at the ceremony for the opening of the new retail market on Tuesday 4 November 1958. People

pressed for a good view of her as she paid tribute to the scale of the changes in the city, and those that were planned for the future. The roof top car park, thought to be the first of its kind in this country, was open and could accommodate two hundred cars. Plans were already in the pipeline for a multi-storey car park adjoining the market. After the ceremony she wandered through the market chatting to stallholders and children playing on a new roundabout. She is reported to have thought this a good idea.

Earlier in 1958, the country was given the news of a tragic aeroplane disaster. A propeller-driven aeroplane crashed in the snow at Munich Airport. Many died in the accident. Aboard were the Manchester United Football club, staff and reporters returning from a European Cup semi-final in Belgrade.

Campaigners for Nuclear Disarmament (CND) marched in London in protest against the plans for American nuclear missile bases in England. Among the key figures in the movement were well known names including Bertrand Russell, Michael Foot, AJP Taylor, John Osbourne and fellow writer, JB Priestley. Security Services and Special Branch kept files on the protestors. 'Big Brother is watching you', was the response from the members of the CND. On Easter Monday in April the first of the marches, which were to become an annual event, took place. They marched to the government's Weapons Research Establishment at Aldermaston.

Wartime

Likely lads they may seem to be as they pose on a pile of rubble in Sandy Lane, but heroes is what they were on the night of the 14 November 1940. Keep your hats on your heads boys, in case of falling rubble as you proceed with the unenviable task of searching through the rubble for survivors.

The Home Guard played a valuable role during the war years. Starting life as the Local Defence Volunteers, they had neither uniforms nor weapons. The locals poked fun and suggested that LDV stood for 'Look', 'Duck', and 'Vanish'. In the beginning they were not taken seriously. Many were older men who were too old to join the regular army. Many had served in the First World War. Some worked in essential occupations and were part-time members of the LDV. In July 1940 their name was changed to the Home Guard. They were attached to local army battalions and were given better equipment. Soon the 'Dad's Army' image faded. They helped build defences, and manned anti-aircraft rocket batteries. They removed road signs to confuse the enemy, should they land on our shores, which caused so much confusion to the local populace that the action was fairly quickly reversed.

Another branch of the civil defence was the ARP (Air Raid Precautions) Officers. Responsible for making sure that not even the slightest light showed, and had the power to impose fines on anyone who contravened the regulations. 'We would be better off with Hitler'. Was the cry that followed them, but those who shouted knew that their work was really essential.

Early morning shoppers outside the City Arcade can receive some useful advice on how to get the best out of their meagre rations at the food advice centre. Recipes were provided at such centres, 'food flashes' appeared on cinema screens with exciting things you can do with your tinned Spam. The BBC broadcasted a 'Kitchen Front' programme at eight fifteen every morning to an audience of about fourteen million people. The welfare of the people had never been given so much attention before. Posters warning everyone that 'Coughs and Sneezes Spread diseases', and offering the advice 'Trap Your Germs in a Handkerchief' were published to 'Help Keep the People Fighting Fit'. The low fat, low sugar, diet, supplemented with fruit and vegetables did more to improve health than any progress in science or the art of medicine. Infant mortality fell and so did the number of people who died from tuberculosis. Children were given their cod-liver oil, quickly followed by the treat of orange juice to take away the taste. To supplement the ration easily grown food, such as carrots were recommended. Every piece of land should be turned over to the production of food. 'Dig for victory', was the campaign's slogan. 'Clara Carrot' and 'Doctor Carrot', who could help you to see in the blackout, appeared on Ministry of Food advertisements. When the milkman's horse had gone by, keen gardeners would rush out to collect the manure in a bucket to fertilise their little kitchen garden. In the better streets there was an unspoken rule that, if the horse left the 'blessing' in area between the invisible lines that extended from your garden walls across the road, then it was yours by right!

Above: There was utter confusion on the morning of 15 November 1940. The police advised workers streaming into the city on foot, to go home and wait until they had further information as to which firms, factories, and shops were still able to operate. Many buildings were in a dangerous condition, and the hard hat hanging from the man's bag would be essential wear. Maybe, like many others on that day, he was offering to search and clear the rubble. First Aid posts were set up in various parts of the city. Communications and essential services had to be re-established. There were still fires that had to be damped down once the water supply was restored. Life had to get back to normal as quickly as possible. There was a determination that, what the Germans were boastfully calling 'The biggest attack in the history of air war', should not defeat them. This was the spirit that was symbolised on the levelling stone laid in Smithford Street, thirteen months to the day after the war ended. The Phoenix, rising from the ashes sums up the mood of the people perfectly. It began on this day. The sailor is a long way from the sea. The navy had their work cut-out for them as they tried to defend the cargo ships bringing much needed supplies from America. They often fell victim to the torpedoes of the blockading U-boats. We all had to accept saccharine in place of sugar, and many children did not know how to open a banana at the end of the war.

Below: Few images reflect the spirit of the people of Coventry better than this. Here the postman follows habit and treads his route. He is a little bewildered at times as to where the letterbox is, and whether his customers have survived the horrors of the previous night. When the sirens wailed out their warning everyone ran to their air-raid shelter, or were directed to one by an Air-Raid Precautions Officer. Later they would emerge as the welcome 'all clear' sounded. There were posters to be seen in many parts of the city advertising 'business as usual' with directions to the temporary premises.

From as early as 1937 the threat of war with Germany was considered a real possibility, and the authorities began to take measures for protection against attack. By 1939 children were evacuated from danger areas to towns designated as 'reception areas'. Gas masks were distributed in 1938. Every man, woman and child was given either a gas mask or respirator to carry with them. Many a boy and girl developed the technique of blowing air gently down the ventilator to make it vibrate and produce a rude, rasping, sound. Sand bags were stacked around police telephone boxes, although in the first raids the land-lines were broken and communications were difficult. The earlier training and preparation then paid off.

Below: When the 'all clear' sounded, after eleven hours of bombing, the people emerged from their shelters to assess the damage. For many their homes had gone, and all their possessions. They had been lucky to be able to take their pets into the cramped, damp, shelters. Shocked and without sleep as the bombs exploded and shook the ground, and the constant pounding of anti-aircraft guns, they are still able to appreciate the hot mug of tea and give a smile of thanks, relieved it is over, and glad to be alive. Over five hundred planes had taken part in that raid on the city. It had seemed that they would never end as they dropped five hundred thousand kilogrammes of high

explosive bombs (1,000,000 lbs), and thirty thousand kilograms of incendiary bombs. What treasures does the girl carry in her shopping bag? The voluntary organisations had practiced and planned for such an eventuality, but they could not possibly have anticipated the scale and severity of the blitz on the city. They were miraculous in the way that they conjured up food and drink for the victims, found shelter, and provided clothes to replace those lost that night.

Bottom: On the 15 November 1940, immediately after the devastating attack on Coventry, the King and Queen Elizabeth made a visit to see, first hand, the situation in which the people found themselves. Mrs Milburn's diary records how, on that morning, there was a knock on the front door of the Mayor's house. Alderman Moseley, the mayor, lived in a small house, in what Mrs Milburn described as, 'one of Coventry's lesser Streets'. The front door was jammed shut due to damage to the building caused by the bombing of the previous night. The Mayor's wife shouted to the people at the door to, 'Come round the back'. When she opened the back door, there stood the King!

The dangers of searching through the rubble are all too apparent as are the need for a bomb shelter of some kind. Various types of shelters were constructed from 1938 onwards. Some surface shelters were built of brick and concrete in public places. Trench shelters were dug in parks and on playing fields. The Government issued Anderson Shelters. These came in corrugated sheets of steel, which had to be bolted together, and dug into the ground to a depth of three to four feet, and then covered with soil. They could withstand quite a lot, short of a direct hit from a bomb, but they were cold and damp, and often flooded in the winter. In 1941 a new type of 'Morrison' shelter was introduced. It was about the size of a table, and was often used for that purpose; made of steel it could withstand the weight of a collapsed building.

When, after a bombing raid on London, Buckingham Palace sustained some damage. The King is reputed to have said, 'Good'. For now that his home had been hit, he felt that he could relate to the people who had suffered in the same way. He and Queen Elizabeth visited the city on the morning following that horrific night in November.

Towers, spires, and chimneys seem to be very difficult for the German bomb aimers to target. The Market hall tower had to be demolished because it was unsafe, but it had stood in defiance of the enemy and resisted their attempts to knock it down. It symbolised the attitude of the people. The rubble has been cleared and the people are back to another 'normality' in 1941, but the

industrial heart of the city has gone. They were, however, left with a 'clean canvas' to begin again once the war was ended. The new would contain many thoughts and innovations in town planning that were revolutionary. The pedestrian precinct was the first of its kind in the country. There were advantages for the motorist who could always find a parking space. There was a 'down-side' too, because they had to watch out for that pothole which could take away the exhaust pipe. Should that happen there was always the bus. After all the posters encouraged everyone to use them and save the valuable fuel. Everything was saved; granny would remove the string from parcels, wrap it around her fingers in a neat skein, and place it safely in a drawer, saying, 'Don't you know there is a war on?'

On the 14 November 1940, Churchill received news that the Germans were preparing for a heavy raid. According to reports, he stood for a time on the roof of a government building waiting for signs of the impending attack. Nothing happened. Bomber Command was tracking large numbers of bombers heading north. The Command Centre in Coventry, located under the post-office in Hertford Street, began tracking bombers heading towards them. The sirens sounded and there was the usual rush for the shelters. It was a 'bomber's moon', a cloudless sky with the moonlight clearly illuminating targets. Blackout restrictions were strict but pointless on such a night. The river and railway lines shone clearly, helping the navigators guide death to the city. Just before seven o'clock the engines of the bombers could be heard, followed shortly by showers of incendiary bombs raining down on the city and setting it ablaze. A seemingly never-ending stream of bombers droned across the night sky. For eleven hours they dropped their deadly load onto the city. A concentrated pattern of destruction the likes of which had never been seen before. People on the ground were helpless. With the water mains destroyed, the firemen could only watch as the cathedral blazed.

Owen Owen's shop, which had opened only three years earlier, is now completely destroyed. The people go about their everyday tasks. Bemused by the scenes of devastation, they try to preserve as much 'normality' as they can. Workers are busy attempting to clear the rubble hoping that they do not find any victims of the raid.

Above: Few had slept the previous night when hundreds of bombers had droned over the city depositing their deadly bombs on the people below. Little remained of the centre and much of the suburbs. A mother drags a confused child along the pavement as she goes in search of any shops still standing, so that she can buy food. Shopkeepers were quick to find alternative accommodation, or to erect temporary premises so that business could continue. They had crawled from their shelters that morning in November 1940, to see what remained of their city, and to get news of their relatives and friends. They moved quietly and business-like around the streets exchanging information. Most other communications were out of action. Those who had radios sat close to them to listen for any news and advice. People who heard the messages were told not to go into the city centre. Many had set off to work as usual. Some cars had got past the policemen who were turning back the traffic on the outskirts, and needed local knowledge to find routes open to their destinations. Gas, electricity and water supplies were cut off.

Top: Outside the 'Coach and Horses', a horse-less carriage may well have seen its last day. The beautiful black paintwork polished to a proud shine, the chrome bumpers now scratched and dented. As if it has been dropped from the skies, it rests nose down. The driver may have been dashing for home, or on official business, and did not see the hole ahead of him. The headlights of cars were fitted with louvered covers to prevent the lights being seen from above. Many road accidents were due to drivers being unable to see the road clearly during the blackout.

The sirens had sounded the warning and the Air Raid Precautions Officers had done their best to ensure that the blackout regulations were observed, but they could not switch off the light of the moon, nor could the firemen extinguish the hundreds of incendiary bombs as they fell that night. They lit the target so clearly for the German bombers. No amount of preparation could have anticipated the experience of that night. Much of Park Street was just one of the many that had the roofs blown off, rubble scattered, windows shattered, and craters excavated. Many historical old buildings were destroyed, but, in some cases, the bombs shook off an outer coating of bricks or mortar to reveal some surprising architectural gems beneath. An example of this is the medieval merchant's house, c1350, in Much Park Street. What was not appreciated at the time was, perhaps, that the change of tactics on the part of the Germans, to attack towns and cities, gave our airfields a chance to recover and prepare to return the compliment.

Living the dream

The word Jaguar today is likely to make most people think, first of all, of a powerful, comfortable, stylish car; or if the animal itself springs to mind, often as not it is sleek and snarling and chrome-plated, leaping forward from back legs anchored to the bonnet of a beautiful, purring car. The marque has been in existence for more than sixty-five years and has built up an enthusiastic following of loyal owners both at home and abroad, and regular meetings are organised by Jaguar owners' clubs. Some of Jaguar's legendary vehicles can be seen in the Jaguar Daimler Heritage Trust museum at Jaguar's spiritual home in the factory in Browns Lane in Coventry, a fascinating motor museum and a fine tribute to Jaguar's founder, Sir William Lyons.

The birth of William Lyons occurred in Blackpool on 4 September 1901, exactly one hundred years ago. As a youngster, he worked for a local car dealer as a salesman, but was above all fascinated by motorcycles, and owned a variety of fast machines. A new neighbour, William Walmsley, shared his passion,

and had started small-scale production of sidecars. The young Lyons bought one of these, and then suggested to Walmsley that they should form a partnership to build and market the 'Swallow' sidecar. They started in business together in 1922, soon after Lyons's twenty-first birthday. The Swallow sidecars with their polished aluminium bodywork proved to be an instant hit.

As a businessman, Lyons was both shrewd and ambitious,

Top: Sir William Lyons.
Above left: An advertisement for one of Lyons' Swallow Sidecars.
Right: The SS1.

and within a few years realised that motorcyclists would eventually replace their bikes with cars. His next step was therefore to bring out a small car. He chose to base his first car on the chassis of the best-selling Austin Seven, which emerged with a stylish special body to Lyons's own design. The first Austin Seven Swallow came on the market in 1927. When the company received an order for 500 cars from Henlys, their distributor in London, Lyons realised that they had to move from the small factory in Blackpool, to bigger premises in the heartland of the motor industry: Coventry.

And so the Swallow company came to Coventry. Lyons found a disused factory off Holbrooks Lane at Foleshill – which later became the Dunlop wheel factory – and moved in the autumn of 1928. Production was gradually increased, and Lyons came into contact with another famous Coventry firm, the Standard company at Canley. Soon Swallow-bodied Standard cars were on the market, and when Lyons decided to make and market his own car, Standard supplied engines and many other parts. The result was the first SSI car, which created a sensation at its launch at the 1931 Motor Show, with its ultra-low body and outrageously long bonnet. It was considered phenomenal value for money - the £1,000 look for £310, as one newspaper reported. The tourer version of the SSI had also brought Lyons his first taste of international competition success, winning the team prize in the 1934 Alpine International Trial in Europe.

For 1938, the SS Jaguar was fitted with a new all-steel body, and for a time Jaguar owned the Motor Panels company. A new larger 3.5 litre engine became available, fitted with this the SS Jaguar 100 could reach 60 mph from standstill in 10.5 seconds, and had a top speed of over 100 mph. This performance put the car in a class of its own at that time, and still for only £445. In the last full sales year before the war, output was more than 5000 cars.

The outbreak of war put a temporary stop to Lyons' developments. However, he had never stopped manufacturing sidecars, and the war brought high demand for sidecars for military use. The company also became involved in aircraft manufacture and repair work, and this introduction to the principles of aircraft design was to prove useful in the future. The factory at Foleshill was just that little bit outside the City to escape the worst of the devastation of the Coventry Blitz, and continued to supply vital material to help Britain's war effort. It was a particular honour to be asked to help building the first British jet fighter, the Gloster Meteor.

The inspiration for the name Jaguar may have come from another Coventry product, a radial aircraft engine made by Armstrong-Siddeley at Parkside during the First World War. In 1935, Lyons was about to take a major step forward with a new range of cars, based on a new chassis with an overhead valve engine of six cylinders and 2.5 litres, and fitted with an elegant four-door saloon body. This car was such a great step forward that he decided it must have a new identity. After having looked at many different names of animals, birds and fish, Lyons chose JAGUAR. The new car was launched at the 1935 Motor Show. At a press reception, Lyons asked the journalists how much they thought the new car was going to cost, and the average of their estimates was £632. Lyons then revealed that the price was just £385! At first Jaguar was a model name, but the marque soon became known as the SS Jaguar. The range also included the first proper sports car, the famous SS Jaguar 100, which came first overall and won the Team Prize in the RAC Rally in 1937.

During the war, Jaguar had bought the tools and rights to the six cylinder engines which had until then still been made for them by the Standard company. Thus a proper machine and engine erection shop was set up in Jaguar's own factory for the first time. While the sidecar division was sold at the end of the war, the company resumed

Top: Launching the SS Jaguar in September 1935.
Below: The company's first proper sports car the SS 100.

manufacture of the pre-war range with the exception of the SS 100 which was not produced again. The emphasis was now on exports, and from 1947 Jaguar cars were made available with left-hand drive! Not surprisingly, however, it was deemed sensible to drop the SS name which had acquired unfortunate connotations. Now the company and the cars were just Jaguar.

The company launched its new post-war model at the 1948 Motor Show, the Mark V which had a new chassis with independent front suspension, and a re-styled version of the pre-war body.

Meanwhile, work had been going on to develop an exciting new engine, the XK, a 3442cc straight six twin overhead cam engine with an output of 160 hp, which Lyons wanted to fit into a new high performance luxury saloon, with a top speed of at least 100mph. Initial design work had been done already during the war, during the famous fire-watching night sessions when Lyons got together with his hand-picked team of engineers, including Bill Heynes, Walter Hassan and Claude Baily. However, the all-new saloon was not ready for production just yet, and as he felt that the

Mark V was not the appropriate car in which to launch the revolutionary new engine, William Lyons decided to design a limited production sports car as a showcase for his new engine. The result was the XK120, considered by many to be the greatest sports car of all time, and a complete show stopper at that 1948 Show.

Labelled as the fastest production car in the world, the sceptics did not believe its advertised top speed of 120 mph, but they were put to shame when an XK120 was timed at 126 mph when tested in Belgium in 1949; with the windscreen removed it even reached 133 mph. In a Production Sports Car race at Silverstone, one of the three XK 120s entered finished first, and another finished second; fortunately for the other competitors, the third had a puncture. Not surprisingly, orders for the car flooded in, especially from the USA which would soon become Jaguar's most important export market, and where Jaguars became the preferred transport of many Hollywood stars, including Clark Gable. It was soon after that the legendary partnership between Jaguar and Stirling Moss was formed, with Moss winning the Dundrod Tourist Trophy in Ulster in his first race in an XK. The XK was also enjoying great rally success, winning the Alpine Rallies

Top: *Whitley Bombers, essential wartime production.*
Above centre: *The XK 120 launched in 1948.*

in 1951 and 1952, in the hands of Ian Appleyard, who in between events also found time to woo and wed William Lyons's daughter, Pat.

The new large saloon finally appeared at the 1950 Motor Show as the Mark VII. Like the XK120 sports car, it was wonderful value for money – both cars had a basic price before tax of just under £1000 – and the performance was everything that Lyons wanted, with a top speed of over 100mph. The model was designed to suit American taste but also found favour in the home market, and other export markets. A particularly distinguished customer was HM Queen Elizabeth the Queen Mother, who gave Jaguar its first Royal Warrant. Many other members of the Royal family also use Jaguars for private or official occasions. The Duke of Kent is a particularly long-standing Jaguar enthusiast.

The new models were so successful that the company had difficulty in meeting the high level of export orders from its existing factory, and began to look around for a new home. After much negotiation with the Ministry of Supply, in 1951 Jaguar rented what was then known as the 'Daimler Shadow Factory No. 2', originally built during the Second World War to manufacture aircraft engines. This became the present Jaguar assembly plant at Browns Lane, Allesley, on the North-Western outskirts of the City. By November 1952, Jaguar was safely installed in its new home, where production over the years would gradually expand from 10,000 to 50,000 cars per year.

Jaguar had now also written itself into the history book of motor sport. The XK120 had put up such a good show in the 24-hour race at Le Mans in France in 1950 that Lyons gave the go-ahead to build a special racing model. This featured a tubular lightweight chassis and aerodynamic bodywork, and was fitted with a tuned XK engine which developed 190bhp. The XK 120C, or the C-Type, had its first outing at Le Mans in 1951; a team of three was entered, two failed to finish (Stirling Moss broke the lap record and was in the lead when an oil pipe flange failed), and the third, driven by Peter Walker and Peter Whitehead, won the race. Two years later Jaguar returned

This page: The elegant 1950 Mk VII Saloon and the poster campaign to promote it.

Jaguar needed now was a smaller, high volume model to complete its range, and this niche was duly filled by the Jaguar 2.4 litre saloon. Introduced in 1955, with a unitary bodyshell and a smaller version of the well-proven six cylinder XK engine, the Jaguar 2.4 provided excellent ride and refinement levels, and remained in production, in one form or another, for almost fifteen years, as the best-selling range of Jaguars until that time. Then in the 1956 New Year's honours list, William Lyons was given a Knighthood for services to export – and perhaps to motor racing! A few weeks later, Her Majesty the Queen and The Duke of Edinburgh paid their first visit to the Jaguar factory.

With the new smaller cars, production was now leaping ahead, and to concentrate all efforts in the business, Jaguar in 1956 decided for a time to retire from motor racing, although the company continued to support private owners

to Le Mans and finished first, second and fourth with C-Types fitted with disc brakes, which were fade-free and so effective that the winning Jaguar became the first car to finish the Le Mans race at an average speed of over 100mph – for twenty-four hours! This important innovation had been developed by Jaguar working in conjunction with Dunlop. Up to then, disc brakes had only been used on aircraft.

Jaguar built 54 C-types and sold most of them to private owners, demonstrating that it was a production car and not just a special racing model. In 1954 the C-Type was replaced by the D-Type, with monocoque construction, tubular front sub-frame and even fuel injection on some of the works racing cars. The D-Type maintained Jaguar's now well-established record in motor racing by winning at Le Mans a further three times – 1955, 1956 and 1957. All

*Top: The C-Type at Le Mans in 1953. **Above:** The D-Type introduced in 1954. **Right:** The Jaguar 2.4 litre saloon, 1959.*

The most famous Jaguar was the E-type which was launched at the Geneva Motor Show in 1961. It combined stunning looks and a top speed of 150mph with a price of little more than £2000. More saloon models were also launched, but all of the older saloons were eventually replaced by the new XJ range which came on the market in 1968 and was an immediate success, offering hitherto unseen standards of refinement and comfort, combined with the traditional Jaguar virtues of elegance and high performance.

This was in other ways a fateful year for Jaguar. Already in 1966, Lyons had agreed to merge his company with Britain's then biggest motor manufacturer, BMC, but in 1968 BMC in turn had to merge with Leyland, creating the British Leyland group, which was effectively nationalised in 1975. Despite the merger causing many difficulties, Jaguar

who took part in competition. A potentially disastrous set-back occurred in the evening of 12 February 1957 when a devastating fire swept through the factory. Nothing daunted, the Jaguar team under Sir William's leadership set about clearing up. Several hundred cars were lost in the inferno, and a large part of the factory had been destroyed, yet within two weeks production had been resumed at half of the previous level. The fire was also a spur to begin a programme of modernising the plant.

In 1959, Jaguar bought the Browns Lane factory outright from the Ministry, but the company was expanding rapidly and was still in need of more capacity. The solution was found in 1960 when Jaguar bought the famous Daimler company which had a large factory at Radford north of the city centre. This eventually became the main engine factory for Jaguar, until it was finally closed down in the 1990s. Jaguar continued making Daimler cars, as an even more luxurious and exclusive version of the Jaguar.

went on to produce another world-beater, the twelve cylinder engine which was introduced in the E-type in 1971, and in the saloon range in the following year.

By then Sir William Lyons had gone into well-earned retirement, after fifty years at the helm of his company. He continued to take a close interest in events at the factory, and remained honorary president of Jaguar until his death in 1985.

A brief period of trouble and production difficulties in the motor industry at the end of the 1970s was successfully overcome. When the Government decided to privatise the

Top left: The devastation caused by the fire in 1957 **Above:** *The 1962 SI 3.8 E-Type.* **Left:** *A 1977 XJ5.3 Coupe.*

company and Jaguar shares were floated in August 1984, the share offer was oversubscribed eight times. Jaguar, in partnership with racing driver and TWR team manager Tom Walkinshaw, was enjoying an era of great competition success in the 1980s. In 1982 Group 44 had designed a sports racing car around Jaguar's V12 engine, and this series, beginning with the XJR-5 and culminating in the XJR-15, continued notching up victories, including Le Mans in 1988 and 1990, and Jaguar won the World Championship for sports cars three times. In 1989, the independent Jaguar company was taken under the wing of the Ford Motor Company, and ten years later became part of the Premier Automotive Group.

Top: The XJR-9 cars which won the 1988 24 hour race at Le Mans. Above: The XJ 220 launched at the 1988 Motor Show.

Meanwhile, Jaguar has continued to enhance its superb range of cars, introducing every conceivable refinement and luxury to ensure that their appeal and competitiveness remain as strong as ever. The E-type had been replaced by the long-lived XJS range in 1975, and this model continued in production for over twenty years. The XJ saloon range went through three generations before being replaced by the new XJ40 in 1986, which in turn gave way to the X300 range in 1994. At the Motor Show in 1988, Jaguar showed a stunning concept car, the mid-engined XJ220, which created so much interest that it was decided to launch it as a limited production model. Billed as the fastest production car in the world, about 280 of these cars were made from 1992 to 1994 in a special Jaguar Sport factory at Bloxham in Oxfordshire, each with an original price tag of £400,000.

At the threshold of the new millennium Jaguar began a period of further expansion. In 1998, Jaguar introduced the mid-range S-Type saloon which is built in the Castle Bromwich factory in North Birmingham, Jaguar's body factory which was originally built to make Spitfires for the Battle of Britain in 1940. Jaguar also returned to motor sport, and for the first time entered Formula 1 Grand Prix racing for the 2000 season. In November 2000 the X-type was announced, a compact sports saloon with 2.5- or 3-litre engines, a state-of-the-art car featuring permanent four-wheel drive. This is the smallest Jaguar for thirty years, and will appeal to a new audience of younger car buyers, who want to join the Jaguar family and share the Jaguar experience. To build this new model, Jaguar took over the factory at Halewood near Liverpool, which was completely re-furbished. While Jaguar was now no longer just a Coventry-based company, Halewood was a symbolic return to the company's original birthplace in the North-West of England. With output already nudging the 100,000 mark, within a few years the X-type will push Jaguar's annual production to double this figure.

So, whether we own a Jaguar or just dream about it, we can look forward to seeing plenty of them on our roads in the future.

In 1988, Jaguar opened a new research and design centre at Whitley, on the South-Eastern side of Coventry. The centre was originally built by Chrysler, but Jaguar has developed and extended the Whitley site, so that it is now one of the most comprehensive automotive design centres in Europe. The 1990s saw a new sports car, the XK8, with a completely new body design, and the new AJ-V8 engine manufactured in the all-new £125 million, dedicated Jaguar facility within the Ford Engine Plant at Bridgend in South Wales. The XK8 was judged 'Best in Show' in Geneva where it was unveiled in 1996, and this model, together with the new V8-engined XJ range, offer today's motorist the very highest standards in their class. Both models became available in 'R' versions with supercharged engines.

*Top left: The XKR. **Above left:** Jaguar's Formula One Grand Prix car. **Below:** The new X-type.*

At leisure

Crowds turned out to enjoy the spectacle at Baginton Airfield on this day in 1959. The Red Arrows acrobatic air team astonished the crowds with their amazing skill and control as they performed their world famous close formation flying. Although seats are provided very few are sitting on them as they strain to get a better view of the team's performance. The row of microphones delivered a commentary to this enthusiastic crowd.

Many of the aircraft on display had been built in the Coventry area, and powered by engines developed in the factories in and around the city. Whitley and the famous Lancaster bombers had been produced by Armstrong Whitworth's plant at Whitley. The Rootes group also built bombers. The Gypsy Moth biplane, some of which can be seen in the line-up of aircraft, was built by Standard, as was every schoolboy's favourite, the Mosquito. Jaguar made bombers and provided parts for several aeroplanes. Daimler's engines were powerful and reliable, and over fifty thousand of them were made during the war years.

Marquee tents and stalls held other attractions. It seems that only one policeman is required to keep order. Standing in a corner of the field he has time to enjoy the exhibition. Those were the days!

Flight of a different kind was in the news in 1959. In September, just before President Khrushchev's visit to the United States, the Russians landed an unmanned spacecraft, the Lunik 2, on the moon. Yuri Gagarin would, in two years time, be the first man in space. Behind the scenes the Americans were training their team of astronauts for a landing on the moon's surface. The 'Space-Race' was well under way!

Below: The swan moves slowly through crowded Broadgate at twenty to five on Pageant day in 1928. No doubt the time is right, as H Samuel's always told the world that theirs were the 'ever right' watches and clocks. There could be a few mums in the crowd who are probably thinking that their daughters would have made a beautiful Festival Queen. Mothers are like that, Al Jolson sang to his 'Mammy' in 1928 in the film 'The Singing Fool'. But today Marjorie Biddulph is the Queen for the day, and is admired by everyone. Flanked by her Maids of Honour, Madge Collingbourne, Edith Varley, Lucy Page, and Lucy Swain, she looks as pretty as a picture. What an honour to have been selected to represent their city. Only one white helmeted policeman in sight to control the crowd on this day. Would that have been possible now? Did people have greater self-discipline then, or is it only because we believe our yesterdays were better? The people in the crowd certainly appear to be smartly

dressed in their suits and hats. Burtons could well have kitted them out for the occasion. The full 'Montague Burton' was a three-piece suit, or the 'Full Monty' as it was then known. A slightly different meaning is given to it today. Following on behind the swan, is an open topped sports car. Isadora Duncan, the dancer, had been strangled to death the previous year, when her scarf became entangled in the wheels of her sports car, but no such unpleasant accidents on this day.

Bottom: Oxford may have sunk in the boat race in this year, but everyone else seemed buoyant. The Festival of Britain heralded a new 'consumer age'. It was a showcase for the best in British industry and innovation. The country was confidently looking to the future. Housewives felt that they deserved a little luxury after the austerity of the war years. Design followed a 'utilitarian' line. Tubular steel furniture with simple lines was all the rage. Plastics took on many shapes and guises. Over the next decade labour saving devices were in demand. The cold cellar with the stone 'keeping' shelf gave way to the more convenient refrigerator. An electric iron could provide heat at the touch of a button. Televisions with small purple screens provided entertainment, whilst an electric kettle boiled the water for the tea. One could listen to 'The Archers' on a transistor radio. A vacuum cleaner, 'that beats as it sweeps as it cleans'. Those who remember 60s television advertisements will be singing the jingle that delivered those words.

The most magical of all was the washing machine, and all the washing powders that promised sparkling, dazzling, white, some with a hint of blue. With the washer pressed against the kitchen sink, mechanically driven rollers would wring the water from the clothes directly down the plughole. Yes you did have to lift the clothes from one compartment to another by hand on the later 'twin tub' model of the late 50s early 60s, but it would spin them dry. The dirty water would run through a pipe hooked over the edge of the sink - what will they think of next? We can't wait to take this display through the streets of Coventry in the Godiva Pageant, and let everyone see.

THE *ELECTRICAL* HOME OF 1951

Above: This Godiva Pageant in 1951 was the first since the war and was organised for the corporation by Mr. Leonard Turner. Sixty tableaux in two sections, 'historical' and 'industrial' wended their way through the streets. It coincided with the Festival of Britain being held on the banks of the Thames. Tony Benn called it 'a decade of hope'.

This Party Political procession is pressing for the election of 'Glynne', and not the Conservative government who have just come to power under the leadership of Winston Churchill. The government of 1951 encouraged the cuts in taxation, which were the start of the first of many consumer booms.

Look carefully at everyone in the crowd. There may be spies lurking there. Britain's diplomatic service is running around in circles after the disappearance of two senior officials from the British Embassy in Washington. So far there has been no news of their whereabouts. They could be mingling with the crowd. There is speculation that Guy Burgess and Donald Maclean could have been spying for the Russians.

Right: 'Daddy, daddy, can we come back next week when the lady has had her hair cut?' 'Just concentrate on keeping your feet on the plank, young man', his father could well be saying. 'All that cod-liver oil and orange juice they are giving him at school is making him too healthy'. Or, as a citizen of Coventry, he is more likely to be telling his son that the lady made this ride to lift the burden of taxes from the grateful people. 'The ride is made with dignity and poise'. Quite why Leofric, Earl of Mercia, should have imposed this embarrassment on his wife is more difficult to explain, but, according to the story, he loved

her and they lived happily ever after, and had Hotels, streets, a cinema, firms and even a fish and chip shop, named after them. It is supposed that the people did not add to her embarrassment, and remained indoors with their curtains tightly closed until she had passed. Later accounts tell of one, a certain Tom, who had to have a peep - the cad! There are a lot of Peeping Toms here today.

It was a great day out for all the family and not a bit of it should be missed, 'Climb up here', was the cry, 'You'll have a better view'. How many modern cars have a roof or bonnet strong enough to stand on without causing permanent damage? Daddy lifts his pretty 'Shirley Temple' look-alike daughter out of her pushchair and, for a time, forgets the difficulties in day-to-day living still being experienced so long after war has ended.

Below: The London actress, Miss Ann Wrigg, aged 28, portrayed the Lady Godiva in 1951. In the eleventh century the ride would have taken only a short time through the village streets, but the Pageant is an afternoon's entertainment, and, unlike the people then who would not look, the pavements are thronging with those who want to get a good view. Ignore the 'No waiting' sign outside the Savings Bank; it is a good vantage point. The crowd are so orderly that children can sit on the kerb side in complete safety. Many are so well organised that they have brought their own chairs. If you are going to do a thing, do it properly.

The horse, a white hunter called Willoughby Warrior, was very restless and needed divine intervention from the nuns, who were there to protect the innocent Lady. It was thought that Willoughby, who was normally a very gentle, docile animal, was proving difficult because of the close proximity of an elephant called 'Sauce'. 'Sauce' and 'Salt' were two baby elephants in the local circus. 'Sauce' carried a model of a tower on its back symbolising the badge of Coventry. The elephant trainer had some problems, it was reported, in persuading 'Sauce' to leave 'Salt', as the partners were rarely separated.

Coventry was one of the largest cities in Medieval England. Its prosperity was based on the manufacture of cloth. The cloth carried a seal of quality to show that it was genuine Coventry cloth. That seal was an elephant. Edward III ensured the prosperity when he passed an act forbidding the purchase of foreign cloth.

Street scenes

'Demolition Sale - all stock must be cleared'. This was the message in every shop in Butcher Row in 1936. Soon the gangs would enter the street and work to raise them to the ground would begin. At the end of the street the notice reads, 'This corner is to be taken away' for 'street Improvement'. Was it improvement? It was done in the name of progress, but is progress the same as improvement?

Whatever the reasons there are many bargains to be had at A W Garlick's Ironmonger's shop. The latest washing equipment is available and it must be cleared. Any future musicians in a skiffle band would have a grand time selecting a well-tuned washboard. What good times were to be had in the 60s rubbing out rhythm with fingers covered with thimbles on a rubbing board. Tea chests were also in great demand. Turned upside down with a hole drilled in the centre to attach a string tied to a broom handle. A skilled performer could apply tension to the string by pulling on the handle and produce an authentic double-bass sound. There are tin baths on display. It was placed in front of the fire on a Friday night, and topped up with hot water from the kettle before it was your turn to get in. Those were the times when a child cursed being the youngest, because they were the last to get into the bath, and when they were dry, they were the ones to put on the 'hand-me-down' clothes.

It seems almost like an act of vandalism to demolish, what is to our modern eyes, such a pretty and interesting street. But in 1936 this fine medieval street was described as 'a slum' and plans were made to clear it and the end result was Trinity Street opened in 1937. The shops display their bargains at the edge of the road in an attempt to clear their stock before vacating the premises. It seems strange to think that the ladies of the time were still doing their laundry with such primitive implements, when in other fields science had advanced so far. The telephone could now tell the time if you dialled TIM. The voice of what sounded like a patient schoolmistress would say, 'At the third stroke it will be three thirty-five precisely. Pip. Pip. Pip.' Mr Mitchell was designing his famous Supermarine fighter plane, later to become the Spitfire, the BBC began transmitting regular television broadcasts, but housewives still swished the clothes in boiling water with a long handled agitator, then passed them, by hand, through a mangle to squeeze out the excess water. They did appear to have some aids to help their daily life. Across the road 'Stovo' was on sale. It mattered a great deal that the iron range, with the fire burning brightly to heat the integral oven, shone with the black polish. It is a matter of pride, as surely as making sure that the front doorstep was clean and scoured with a yellow stone.

The demolition contractors are at work in the High street in 1937. Little did they know that the German bombs would remove most of the buildings in this area in a matter of hours only three years hence. The Gaumont was to vanish, and so did the 'Rex' in Corporation Street, which was newly opened in the year that this picture was taken. A bomb hit it in August 1940, just the week before it was to screen the epic film, 'Gone With the Wind'. What a sad loss the picture palaces were. Do you remember the days when we queued at the matinée on Saturday? Only a few pence to see Tom Mix ride into town and save the damsel held by the evil bank robber, or Roy Rodgers, who was not only fast on the draw, but sang like an angel. There was always the serial, at the end of which the heroine or hero was about to be cut in half by a circular saw, with no means of escape. Flash Gordon could be trapped in a room with poisonous gas entering, when a voice asked, 'Is this the end of Flash Gordon? Has the evil Ming succeeded? Come back next week and find out!' We worried all week, but the escape was nearly always an anti-climax, which brought hoots of laughter from the audience. And when the film broke and the theatre lights were turned on, which was a fairly regular occurrence, there were loud whistles and hoots and calls to the projectionist to 'Put a shilling in the meter'. When the lights dimmed once more a cheer went up and the whole audience counted down as numbers appeared on the screen heralding a new start to the film.

There can be no prettier place than this sun-dappled ancient street, which is, surprisingly, only a short distance from the busy centre of the city. There is time to stop and stare or have a conversation with a passing neighbour. 'Stress' is a modern concept, which does not exist here. Numbers three, four and five are rare sixteenth century, or possibly earlier, buildings. These cottages in Priory Row were once known as the Lychgate Cottages. The word 'lych' means corpse. As you can guess, the gate opposite was the entrance to the graveyard through which the coffin would be carried. The church on the left is Holy Trinity Church where one of Coventry's most famous residents, Mary Ann Evans was a member of the congregation.

Better known as the author George Elliot, she adopted this pseudonym because she thought that her books might be more readily accepted if the world thought her to be a man.

Over the wall to the right of the photographer are the Cloister gardens. Once this was the site of St Mary's Priory, founded by Earl Leofric. Legend has it that there are many crypts and tunnels beneath the banking, wherein lie the bodies of the Earl and Lady Godiva. This is the very stuff from which an Enid Blyton mystery, involving the Famous Five, might spring. It may or may not be true, but it would make a grand tale. Many buildings at the end of the Row were demolished to make way for the construction of Trinity Street.

Preparations are underway in Broadgate for the visit of Princess Elizabeth in May 1948. The stand is in the process of erection and traffic queue to pass through the single lane. Queuing has become second nature to everyone in Britain. Bread came off ration in this year, but clothes continued to be rationed, along with sweets, until 1949. Milk rationing continued and the allocation was reduced to two pints per person per week in 1949. Neither Princess Elizabeth nor Lady Godiva are due to arrive yet. The famous lady, riding on her horse will take pride of place in the centre of the green next year. Soon, in a matter of four short and interesting years, the Princess will be riding sidesaddle as she officiates at the trooping of the colours in place of the king who was too ill to attend. In a short time following this event, she will become Queen. Her Empire is in a state of change, India gained independence the previous year and, four months earlier, the Indian leader Mahatma Gandhi had been assassinated whilst walking in New Delhi.

Below: Owen Owen were now in temporary premises, their other shop having been destroyed in the early years of the war. But, like other businesses large and small, it was back to work as quickly as possible. Not wishing to lose faithful customers, they had quickly found other accommodation or constructed corrugated iron or pre-fabricated ones. 'Open as usual' signs became symbolic of the attitude of the period. Phrases like, 'You can't keep a good man down', entered conversation with strength of meaning which they never had before. It does not seem surprising that Lego bricks should have been invented at this time.

There is plenty of time to cross the wide expanse of Trinity Street, even though the 50s and 60s were 'boom years' for the car industry in Coventry, the road is quiet. The population increased in 'Car City' to just over 300,000, of which 60,000 worked in the motor industry. The planners had great foresight in anticipating and preparing for the future growth in traffic. These were the years when the Highway Code was published by a concerned government, who issued a copy with every provisional licence applied for, or every licence on renewal. The general public could have one for the princely sum of one penny.

Bottom: The bus turning into Hearsall Lane may be carrying workers returning from the Standard Motor Company, at Canley. Standard Triumph built cars there from 1914 to 1980. British Leyland, who had taken over the production of the cars in 1968, undertook a rationalisation programme and the name disappeared. When this picture was taken the company had not yet reached the height of expansion. That occurred in the sixties. The Triumph Herald, which according to the advertisements of the time, 'could run rings around a London taxi', was built in the new 'Rocket Range' assembly building. One of the last production cars to be built on a chassis, this versatile car really did have an incredible turning circle. The entire bonnet lifted to give easy access to the engine for ease of maintenance.

The old lampposts had a personality. They were, somehow more than just a means of light, but became the place to meet friends. 'See you on the corner under the lamp,' was the young lover's call. George Formby sang as he was 'leaning on a lamppost at the corner of the street in case a certain little lady' passed by. To help pass the time he could call for two ounces, or if the money and ration coupons were sufficient, a quarter of 'Pear drops', 'Poor Bens' or maybe Liquorice 'torpedoes', or 'aniseed balls'. The shopkeeper would weigh them, lift the brass dish from the scales, and tip them into a paper bag. With a deft spin, the corners of the bag would twist to hold the contents securely in place.

It is strange how our modern eye changes this view of the backs of poor cottages on Spon Street into a picturesque scene of children engaged in innocent play. Like them, we no longer see the neglect, but instead the plants growing from the roof, the brick path and walls, and the irregular windowpanes, all add texture and interest to this charming picture. The brick path would also lead to the outside privies, no doubt. It was the source of many a music-hall comedian's jokes. It was no joke to the residents in the winter months, when members of the family had to carry a lantern to light their way. The striped Fair Isle pullover that Mum had knitted was much appreciated in a house with no central heating or double-glazing. The bits of coloured wool carefully unravelled from an older garment. Children always loved to pull the thread and watch as the old cardigan disappeared. Our mothers and grandmothers taught the skill of wrapping the wool around the fingers to produce a small skein around which the rest would be twisted to produce a tight ball. When there was enough they would be combined with others to produce the familiar horizontal striped pattern.

Spon Street escaped serious damage during the bombing, but this area underwent major changes in the 50s and 60s as the area was redeveloped. Many medieval houses were demolished to build blocks of flats. Others disappeared as the ring road cut a path around the city.

Above: Could this be the hero 'Ernie' who, according to Benny Hill, 'drove the fastest milk-cart in the West? There was no mention in the song that he worked for the Co-op. He certainly will not be speeding on this day in the 60s. Not with a road surface as wet as this one here in Mill Race Lane, Bell Green. During the war years he had to drive where he was told to go as the government introduced a 'zoning' scheme. Housewives woke up one morning to find they had a different milkman, whistling a different tune. The idea was to make better use of the resources by making the system economically more efficient. Whether that was the case or not will never be known, but it did demonstrate the speed with which the government of the time could introduce any changes that they thought necessary.

Houses, such as the ones seen here, are typical of the style adopted in the 50s and 60s, when houses were needed for the growing population of Coventry. Lessons in the prefabrication of windows and doors were quickly learned. Mass production brought down the cost. The metal window frames did cause condensation, and good ventilation was the answer. Building materials were controlled and the builder required a licence, before work could commence.

After the Clean Air Act was passed in July 1956, smokeless fuel replaced coal and coke. How many can remember the job of emptying the ash-box every morning, or the skill of rolling newspaper into tight sticks to start the fire? An under-floor flue delivered a controllable jet of air and made the fire burn brightly. Some even provided heat to a fire back boiler for the hot water system and partial central heating. Dad had to get

up early on a cold winters morning to light the fire before the rest of the family climbed from their warm beds.

Below: Looking south down Foleshill Road in 1949 traffic is sparse. The chap on his motorcycle and sidecar does not see the need to wear a crash helmet or to have markings on the road to keep him to his own side. He would have been glad that his bike would give him more miles to the gallon than the car ahead of him as petrol increased in price from September 1949. Because Britain was in debt to both Canada and America, the pound was devalued by over thirty percent. This meant that many of the things, such as butter, which were no longer rationed, were beyond the means of many families. Beyond the wall with the damaged hoardings, the Coventry canal runs to the canal basin past the Electric works. The Standard Motor Company set up premises near the canal basin. The Daimler Motor Company established premises in the 'Motor Mills' in Sandy Lane, as their premises at Much Park Street proved inadequate as the company expanded. Many a boy has escaped the watchful eye of his mother to go down to the canal bank with his net and jam-jar in the hopes of catching a fish. Who taught him to tie a string around the neck of the jar to make a carrying handle? There always seemed a hope that today was the day when they would 'bag' a newt. The small creatures never seemed to live long after they were held in captivity. Neither did the goldfish, received in exchange for old clothes when the rag and bone man shouted in the street, or those won at the fair and carried home in a plastic bag full of water.

Above: It is the late 50s and windows need to be cleaned at numbers 167, 168, and 169 Spon Street. Approximately ten years after this picture was taken, the Townscape plan was launched, and number 169, seen in this picture before it was restored, was the first building to receive attention. Much of the character of early buildings was hidden beneath cement and pebble dashing. Number 169 is one of the oldest buildings in the street, and restoration revealed distinctive curved braces on the front of the building. This was once a centre for dyers and tanners. It was established outside the city walls because of the use of noxious substances used in the processes, and a need for a constant source of running water. The silk trade in Coventry declined, but watch makers set up their factories and the area continued to thrive.

Down on the ground one of the most sensible and reliable forms of transport was the very popular Morris Minor 1000. The one seen here is the earlier model with a split windscreen. Soon the ability to form the screen into a curved shape would replace it, and the centre strut would no longer impair the driver's view.

Right: Under the shadow of the gas works, on this sunny day in the sixties, the ladies may well be debating future plans for the city's ring road. Hill Street was on the planned path. Ringway Hillcross sliced its way through at about this point.

The top houses, with the rows of windows to provide maximum light, are some of the 'top shops' to be found in the Street. The weavers worked on this floor to produce the silk ribbon, for which Coventry was at one time famous. With the gradual end to the trade because of cheap imports from abroad, the trade in watch making replaced it as a cottage industry. The traditional system had been one where the manufacturers bought the rough made watch parts from the 'top-shop' workers and employed specialists to finish and assemble them. The steam-powered factories soon ended this inefficient system, and the workers found the adjustment to working 'to the clock' a difficult one to accept. The watch manufacturer, Richard Day rang a bell to get them to work on time. At the bottom of Hill Street today is Leigh Mills car park. Only the name now marks the textile Mill that once stood here.

These railings have survived the collection of metal for the war effort. Many people returned from the cinema or the pub to discover that their railings had been cut off and carted away to help 'the war effort'. Many gave them up happily feeling proud to have been able to contribute. Every little, they thought, brought the end of the war nearer, and the return of their sons and husbands. The truth was that much of the metal gathered, including the scarce aluminium from our pots and pans, was never used.

Below centre: Shopping was always done at a gentle pace in the 50s, and arcades are such pleasant places. Traffic is not a problem, and there is time to browse in the shop windows. The sunlight streams in through the glass arched roof as the shoppers look for bargains. These were the days when bargains were to be had, and 'sales' were genuine opportunities to save a few pence. This was a time for a little pampering, all the adverts told you so. It was an age when selling became an art. Door to door salesmen were soon appearing in Britain as they had in America. By the end of the 50s and into the 60s, for a few shillings 'down', and a few bob per week, it was possible to buy anything. In the 60s it was called the 'never-never', and it became so easy to fall into serious debt. Granny and mother frowned and piously, and pointed out that it was better to save and own the goods. Filmmakers extolled the same virtues, 'Live now-Pay later'. Someone famous or expert always endorsed products. Toothpaste recommended by dentists or a film star would sell better. Soon there would be self-service, which was difficult to accept by a generation brought up on, 'You don't touch it until you have bought it!' They were accustomed to personal attention, and patiently waited for their turn and made the most of it when it came.

Below: This time it is not the work of an enemy that has levelled the buildings to the ground, but the ever increasing demands of traffic. The plan, to create a pedestrianised centre to the city, was in advance of its time. It was copied throughout the world. The buildings in the original precinct are now listed. The planners realised that the traffic, vital to the rapidly expanding industry of the area, would consequently be pushed to the outskirts, and had to flow smoothly. Before the ring road was completed, there were 146 cars per 1,000 of the population. Half as many again as the national average of 107. This queue of drivers may well have been complaining about their journey, but when the inner ring road was ready they would move in greater numbers to the link roads which would carry them to their destinations, Birmingham, Warwick, and Leicester, with relative ease. This morning trek to work would not be necessary if only the Littlewood's promise would only come true. The collector at the door took the coupon every week, and, for only a few pence it was possible to win half a million! With that you could buy the Admiral Lord Rodney, and one of the best of the cars your days were spent building at the factory. A holiday on the island of Capri with Gracie Fields, the Lancashire Nightingale, and you would still have plenty of cash left over. If only. But for now a more realistic dream may be to save up sufficient to buy a little Morris Minor. Looking quite modern in shape, as it waits, next but one in line, behind the bus. When it first appeared in 1948, the two-door saloon cost £280. By 1961, the year the millionth sale was achieved, it cost £416.

'Every cloud has a silver lining', according to the saying. When incendiary bombs destroyed the cathedral in 1940, the terrible tragedy seemed to have no bright side whatsoever. But when decisions were taken to build a new cathedral great artistic opportunities were created. It could not be built on the site of the old St Michael's for that had now become a beacon shining forth defiance to an enemy, and resolve to rise and rebuild. The mere placing together of two charred roof beams in the form of a cross, or the act of tying two ancient iron nails to form a simple crucifix, the making of an alter of broken stones all expressed a spirit and strength that words alone could not do. It had to be new. The competition brought together the finest artists and architects of the period. When the King and Queen Elizabeth had visited in April 1951 the Provost told the 'Evening Telegraph' that they had shown great interest in the competition. Four short years later work began on the design by Sir Basil Spence. After the opening in May 1962, thousands of visitors from all over the world made the pilgrimage to see it, and the queue has never ended. As they move along from the coaches, which can be seen parked row upon row, they pass Epstein's sculpture of the winged St Michael overcoming the Devil at the doorway. This building has already achieved the status of a grade one listed building.

The spire of the old Cathedral of St Michael stands alongside that of Holy Trinity Church, having miraculously survived. It had been built with firm foundations in the ground, and not, as in many, from the roof of the main building. Once, before becoming a cathedral, it had been the largest parish church in England. Now it has grown into a symbol of reconciliation.

Below: As the people go about their business beneath the tower of the market in the centre of Coventry on this morning they could not possibly envisage that all of these buildings would disappear in a single night. There were warnings from Mr Churchill that the Germans were preparing themselves for war, but that seemed so distant. They were too busy working hard to recover from a depression, and whole country hoped that these rumours were untrue. They had already fought 'the war to end all wars'. These were peaceful times.

In the 30s you could leave your bicycle in safety and expect it to be there when you returned. It could be a tricky and dangerous ride over the cobblestones. Not only would they give a shaky ride, but a dangerous one when the ground was wet. The road surface was not the only hazard for the cyclist, for the tramlines, if not crossed properly, would take charge of the front wheel and throw the rider.

When the Market Tower was to be demolished because it was unsafe, the mechanism was taken to operate the puppet clock in Broadgate. When King George and Queen Elizabeth visited Coventry in 1951, they were shown the animated model of Lady Godiva and Peeping Tom, who were to be featured in the clock on the bridge over Hertford Street. Lady Godiva, he was told, will make an appearance for ten seconds every hour. On hearing this, the King is reported to have commented that he hoped it would not create any traffic problems when the naked lady appeared.

On the move

others were suspicious of bread that was 'wrapped and sealed'; it seemed somehow 'artificial'. Maybe this was the modern way and more hygienic, but wasn't it casting a criticism at all those who still made their own. The kitchen smelled sweet on baking day. Has there ever been a taste to beat that of freshly baked bread? Our noses went in the air in the same way as the nose of the little boy who could smell the gravy salts from a mile away. 'Ah Bisto'.

The tram rumbled on to the end of the track, with the occasional 'loop' in the track to allow his partner to pass. At the terminus the driver disconnected the control handle and carried it to the other end. As he walked down the tram he would swing the backs of the wooden seats over so that the passengers faced the way they were going. The conductor (now there is a word no longer heard today) slid a long bamboo pole with a hook on the end from the tube beneath the tram. He hooked it into a ring situated beneath the pantograph, that arm which made contact with the overhead cable, and swung it through one hundred and eighty degrees until it faced the opposite way ready for the return journey. It always sparked as it parted from its power source on frosty days. The driver would take his watch from the pocket of his waistcoat, and time the return trip to coincide with his fellow tram driver. When bombs destroyed the tramlines they were not replaced and they glided through the streets of Coventry no more.

Centre: Old properties and narrow streets give way to the new wider thoroughfare demanded by the motorcar, lorry, and bus. As the people stroll across the road, protected from the traffic by two lines of studs, it is clear that courtesy and consideration were all that were needed. The studs follow the most direct line from one road to the other, rather than the shortest distance across the road. Modern attitude expects the pedestrian to walk further and inconvenience the motorist as little as possible. More land has been cleared than the road required and is advertised behind the hoardings. Anyone buying it would have had but a short time to benefit from the purchase as this picture was taken in 1939, and one year later the work of creating this new road was gone. Luckily many of the historic buildings further up Hill Street survived both bombs and town planners. St John's Church stands on the corner of this junction. This church served Bablake College, a community of priests. When the college fell into disuse, a school for poor boys was founded using part of the college buildings with slight modifications. The school still remains along with the almshouse known as Bond's Hospital. During the Civil War Scottish prisoners were housed in the church, and in the surrounding area. Because they were shunned and despised, and the people would not speak to them, the phrase, 'being sent to Coventry', came into being.

Bottom: Coventry may well be called 'Motor City', for many of the most famous names in the history and development of the motorcar began here. Harry J Lawson is credited with having founded the motor industry in the city. In 1896 he bought Widdrington Mill, in Drapers' Fields, and renamed it 'Motor Mills'. He bought the patent rights from Léon Bollée for his motor tandem. The first one made in Britain caused a problem, so the story goes, when they tried to drive it out of Motor Mills it would not start. It was decided that they should change the petrol and filled the tank with benzene, whereupon it started first time and they drove out of the Mill and took a trip to Leamington. He was fortunate that the 'Emancipation Act' was passed that very year allowing him to drive on the road without a man with a red flag leading the way. This Highways Act was sensible at a time when most vehicles on the road were horse drawn and the horseless vehicles were very often steam powered and very noisy. The man with the flag gave riders and coachmen time to calm their horses before they steamed past at two miles per hour in the town and a breathtaking four miles per hour in the country.

The first lady sits in a very vulnerable, but apparently comfortable position, with her feet tucked behind the curved dash panel. The advertisements for the Pennington Autocar proudly boasted that, 'It will not blow up and passengers do not run the risk of being set on fire'. 'It can run up hills without emitting smoke or steam and it can run over tram lines at any angle in perfect safety'. These are just a small sample of the variety of machines produced by the proud car manufacturers of Coventry.

Below: Looking east along White Street there is a chimney standing proud. Having dodged the worst of the war years it is one of the last of many which once belched smoke into the air in this industrial heartland. Like the others it carried the smoke high into the sky as power was generated for the City Flour Mill. Tall though they were, the smoke was not always carried clear. In certain weather conditions the smoke combined with the fog and the new word 'smog' was coined. It could be difficult to see more than a few feet ahead on such days, and hair and clothes would be covered with a thick sooty deposit. Pressure on the government for clean air meant that they had to act. In the 'great smog' of 1953 hundreds of people in London contracted heart and lung diseases as a result. From 1953 smog masks were available on the NHS. The Clean Air Act was passed in 1956 and came into force two years later. Now the air is clear enough to see that 'Guinness is consumed by five million people per year' on a poster at the bottom of the road. It is 'Good For You', was the claim, and the figure, in this clever advertising campaign, and gradually rose to seven million.

On this day in 1960 the sun shines brightly and the happy bride in the newspapers in this year was Princess Margaret, who married the photographer, Anthony Armstrong-Jones. The photographers, who have the foresight to record such scenes, must receive our gratitude, for soon the ring road will cut its way through this area, and without their images the past is lost.

Right: He may well have inspired the author of 'On the Buses', to invent the character 'Blakey'. Having wound the sign to give the correct destination and got the crew off on time, his other task was to check that all passengers had the correct ticket. We were in trouble if the fare stage had passed. Ranking as one of the oldest riddles in history is, 'Why is it that you have to wait a long time for a bus, then three come at once?' 'Have your fares ready please', was the familiar cry from the conductor, those people who have become as extinct as the dinosaur. With their ticket dispenser slung diagonally across in one direction and the leather money bag in the other. Children collected bus tickets, as they did with stamps, cigarette packets, and cigarette cards. They were 'swapped' in the school playground. The forerunners of Pokemon, and considered equally valuable, they have now even achieved 'antique' status. Many of the old buses served as auxiliary ambulances during the blitz. Romances began by 'chance' meeting on the top deck. It was a legitimate way to sit next to a pretty girl and engage in conversation without raising eyebrows.

That famous winged 'D' of Daimler, grew in the 'Motor Mills', a disused cotton mill at Sandy Lane. Harry J Lawson, a local entrepreneur who owned the Humber Cycle Company, bought the building and founded the Daimler Motor Company. With a work force, whose skills were easily adapted from the making of cycles, he began constructing cars.

Centre: There were more building sites and scaffolding in Coventry after the war than in any Spanish holiday resort. The bridge, at the top of Hertford Street, is now absorbed into the building of the new pedestrianised shopping area.

When the war ended, there was an expectation that everything would be as it had been before. There was a shock for some, when rationing, not only of certain food and clothing, but of the raw materials needed for building and industry continued. It may seem surprising that not everyone wanted it to end quickly. In the 'letter bag' of the Coventry Evening Telegraph on 6 July 1951, a lady was complaining about the shortage of coke and was dreading the coming of the winter months. She, and others, had to be 'registered', but there was no coke to be had. She argued for the return of rationing, because, even if the amount received was small, there was a guarantee of getting some! New building techniques were employed. Prefabrication of parts in factories and delivered to building sites meant that buildings could be erected quickly to replace the hundreds of houses, offices, and factories destroyed by the bombing. Although they were the butt of many music-hall jokes, people found the 'prefab' houses to be cosy and comfortable. Although they were originally intended as temporary accommodation, many were kept for more years than had been planned. In 1953 you could listen to a new transistor radio in your warm comfortable 'prefab', or enjoy the witty Lady Isabel Barnett, then only 33 years old, guess the occupation of a contestant on the TV show 'What's my line?'.

Bottom: 'Heaven' was sitting on the embankment with a friend during the school holidays collecting train numbers. There was always the possibility that a 'namer' would come by. They bellowed smoke and hissed steam in a way that seemed to give them life. They were full of 'attitude'. We always hoped it would be the 'Flying Scotsman'. First known as 'The Special Scots Express' it changed its name. When the name changed is uncertain, but it happened when the Great Northern Line was bought by L.N.E.R. This train stirred our imaginations as it roared from London, King's Cross to Edinburgh pulling eight twelve wheeled cars. A Pullman refreshment coach was added in the early sixties. It broke all records of the time. If an inanimate object can be a hero, it was our hero in a way that these Diesel engines never could. Even decorated in their smart green livery, powered by a Rolls Royce engine, and sporting the 'whiskers' of the Midland Railway, it could never replace the old steam powered engine in our hearts. The end of an era had arrived when no more were made after 1960. The Government's rescue plan for the railways began in 1955, with over one thousand six hundred million pounds injected over a period of fifteen years. It had come just a little too late. Roads were improving. The M1 motorway opened in 1959 and bus operators were quick to realise the speed advantages, although not faster than the train, were getting close, and they could offer cheaper fares.

Making a living

The groom clings on to the nervous horse as the steamroller hisses and rumbles forward crushing the base foundation for the road. Steamrollers were a common sight in 1919, but were in continual use right into the 1940s. The acrid smell of smoke and the pungent fumes of the tar can be imagined as we stand and watch the men at work. They were lucky to be in employment, as it is only one year after the war had ended and there were thousands of able-bodied men without jobs to go to. Almost as if they were still in uniform, they all wear collarless shirts held closed at the neck with brass collar studs, and their waistcoats and caps. With a stud at the back, and the one at the front, a collar and tie could be quickly attached and a chap could them look smart in an instant. Without it he would not have been allowed into the Savoy, further down the street, for one of their luncheons or afternoon teas. Assuming that he had sufficient money to pay in a time when strikes were occurring regularly. Pay was poor, and there was general unrest in the land. Shirts needed fewer washes if a plentiful supply of collars was available. Collars and cuffs were the parts of a shirt that wore out quickest, so it was very sensible to have detachable ones. At weekends, when one waistcoat pocket held his heavy silver watch secured to a buttonhole with a chain and fob, he would place something heavy in the opposite pocket to balance the waistcoat and hold it level.

Above: It should have been 'the war to end all wars', but it wasn't. The first world war changed warfare forever. At the start officers rode into battle on horseback, and there was a strange notion of 'honour'. These ideas fell as quickly as the infantry men who were faced with a new machine gun. The tank moved to attack with surprising speed and deadly effectiveness, and the glory of charging cavalry was ended. Poems now spoke of the futility of war rather than its glory. Shells like the ones in the Daimler factory at Coventry were delivered considerable distances by massive guns with devastating effect. Young men, inadequately trained, were on the receiving end. It is said that, in the final 'push' against Germany in 1918, the majority of foot soldiers were teenagers. At sea the submarine sent silent torpedoes to sink ships with one blow at the cost of many lives. When a slow moving air-ship sailed silently over London, the streets were lit and life was proceeding as normal, after all the war was raging 'somewhere else' many miles away. They were appalled by 'this cowardly act' when bombs were dropped upon the defenceless people below without the courtesy of a warning! That was bad enough, because one could shoot at a slow moving Zeppelin, but when fast bi-planes, which could carry up to six one hundred and ten pound bombs, dropped them on civilians that was 'simply not cricket'! The new terror now was that, from this day forward, there was no place safe, and civilians could and would be killed. The passenger ship 'Lusitania' torpedoed with many people on board, but it was also carrying much needed supplies, and was, therefore, considered a 'fair' target.

Wars are not won only on the battlefields, but also in the factories. Like ants swarming over the factory floor c1916, these men were winning the war as sure as if they were on the battlefields of the Somme. Many skilled workers were compelled to work in the factories making the necessary guns and ammunition, despite the fact that they would have wished to serve in the armed forces. The skills they used in peacetime were turned to provide the needs of war. Just like the 'Bevin Boys' of the second world war, they were the essential, unsung, heroes. When there were insufficient men to go into the engineering works and down the pits to bring out the fuel essential to 'The War Effort', Bevin selected them from the call-up lists by ballot. Posters gave the message 'Every blow we strike needs fuel'. These factories needed fuel to produce these massive guns. The women had always had a clear role defined for them. They were the homemakers. They were mothers and wives first and foremost, until the factories were desperate for workers to keep pace with the demands of the war, then their duty was redefined. Posters cried out for the women of Britain to come into the factories. They were retrained. They joined the Women's Voluntary Service. They worked on the land in their familiar Khaki and green uniforms as land-army girls. They 'dug for victory' in the gardens and fields, producing scarce food. They delivered the post, collected the fares on the buses, and they worked in the foundries and factories. They were not ready to slip quietly back, when the conflict ended, they had found independence, and would never be willing to relinquish it.

New development and expansion for Coventry station are underway. The city was linked to London and Birmingham by rail in 1838. The track followed the route, which had been suggested by George Stephenson, who is said to have walked the route three times.

Coaches and cars wait for the passengers to arrive and take them on the rest of their journey until the improvements are completed, but many such improvements came a little too late for much of the rail network. Although the government injected a vast sum of money into their development, they were facing stiff competition from road transport in the 50s and 60s. Roads had improved and petrol rationing had ended. People had more money to spend and car ownership was set to double in the next twenty years. A family car was much more convenient, and soon there would be a startling new phenomenon, the Mini. The first motorway to be opened was the Preston Bypass, in December 1958, and the first section of the M1 in 1959. The building of the motorways lessened the speed difference between road and rail travel, and the coach companies were quick to exploit it. They could offer the guarantee of a reserved seat, whereas the railway could not. Then along came Dr. Beeching, later to become Lord Beeching, who decided that there were many branch lines, and small railway stations that were losing money - and so down came the Beeching axe! Two thousand, one hundred and twenty eight stations were closed in 1963, and over a quarter of the track.

Above: Buildings stand as an island in a sea of muddy waves cut by the wheels of a mechanical bulldozer, as the shafts and footings are excavated for the foundations of Lanchester College. The steel rods are waiting for the wooden mould to encase them before the concrete is poured. Soon the much needed university buildings would be ready to cater for the growing demand for places. With the end to national service, there was no break in the move from child to adult. Young men no longer received call-up papers, requiring them to join the armed services, shortly after leaving school. They could keep their long 'quifs' of hair, pushed into shape and held in place with a little 'Brylcreem'. Their hair would no longer be swiftly cut away by the army barber into the 'short-back-and-sides' style acceptable to the sergeant. Now they had the freedom to grow their hair as they pleased. Mothers continued to cover the backs of the armchairs with a white lace-edged antimacassar, even though the Brylcreem advert claimed that it was 'emulsified' for 'clean grooming', it could still leave a greasy patch on furniture. Lanchester is a name that became well known in the city. FW Lanchester was born in 1868, and grew to become an engineer with flare and imagination. He was involved in projects to do with aerial flight and acoustics. In 1901 he designed a car that carried his name and was renowned for its silent, smooth, running. Daimler took over the company in 1931, but sensibly retained the name 'Lanchester' right up to 1956. Lanchester became chief engineer for Daimler and died in 1946.

Coventry calling the World

Telephones, radio the internet. Many of us may not have quite got the hang of the internet just yet, but we are all familiar with the first two, even if the older ones amongst us still persist in calling our radios 'the wireless'.

Once very few of us had the privilege of having a telephone in our own homes. More often than not a telephone call meant a walk to the red phone box down the street, making sure we had enough pennies for the call and carefully reading the instructions about pressing button A or B. How many kids never, ever, missed the chance of pressing button B in the hope that some poor soul had forgotten to collect their coppers after leaving the phone box? Come to that how many readers tried blocking the hole up with paper to stop the money coming back in the hope of making a financial killing later in the day?

As children most of us didn't spend much time thinking about how telephones actually work, having progressed no further in our understanding of 'telecommunications' technology than a length of waxed string connecting two tin cans. Other children however perhaps knew rather more, especially if their fathers or mothers had worked for Coventry's Marconi or its predecessor companies.

Communication at a distance has been an ambition of the human race since time immemorial. Runners, and horsemen were fast but never fast enough. Only the speed of light - 186,000 miles per second - would ever give the illusion of instant communication.

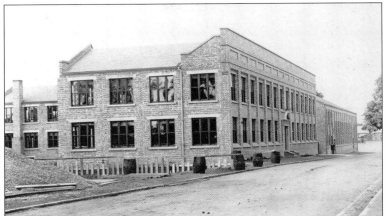

Signal fires ready to give news of the Spanish Armada would in effect provide information at exactly that

Above: The original Peel Corner site.
Below: A view of the original site in the 1920s.

transmitted a message in his famous dot dash code along a telegraph cable in the USA and the age of electric communication hurtling data along copper wires at almost the speed of light was truly with us.

In 1858 the first transatlantic telegraph cable was laid enabling instantaneous communication from Europe to the USA, several decades before the first transatlantic telephone cable.

Almost twenty years after the laying of that first Atlantic cable a teacher of deaf children, the British scientist and inventor Alexander Graham Bell, famously invented the telephone, patenting his revolutionary invention in 1876.

Despite being rightly thought of as the inventor of the telephone Bell's invention would not have been as

speed, but they hardly provided much detail. Semaphore flags would do better. In 1794 in revolutionary France Claude Chappe built a system of Windmill sized semaphore stations from Marseilles to Paris, with the English following soon after with a similar system linking Portsmouth and the Admiralty in London.

Semaphores and heliographs worked well in daylight but failed miserably at night and in fog. In 1839 Charles Wheatstone and William Coke in England devised the first electric telegraph. Four years later Samuel Morse

Top, both pictures: *Staff in the 1920s.*
Right: *A Peel Corner Telephone Works vehicle at the goods entrance to the Peel Corner site.*

immediately successful as it was had it not been for the work of the American Thomas Alva Edison (1847-1931) co-inventor of the electric light bulb and whose contribution to the telephone would be the carbon transmitter, a type of microphone, which when added to the Bell telephone would vastly improved its performance.

Both electric telegraph and telephone would rely on many millions of miles of wire. Gugielmo Marconi (1874-1937) the Italian-Irish inventor would however pioneer wireless telegraphy - radio as we would call it today. By 1895 he had achieved wireless communication over more than a mile. In England the following year he conducted experiments that led to the formation of the company that became Marconi's Wireless Telegraphy Company Ltd, sharing the Nobel Prize for physics in 1909.

Now at the beginning of a new millennium the last few decades have witnessed information and communications applications and networks transforming the world: people have become able to talk with one another or access and share information from almost anywhere on the

Both pictures: Two more views showing typical working conditions during the 1920s.

planet. That pace of change will continue for several more decades as networks become faster and provide many more features. People everywhere will eventually have instant access to high speed, high quality and very low cost connections to friends and colleagues and to expertise and information in a way we can scarcely comprehend today.

Communications is one of the fundamental advances that changed the face of the 20th century. Its

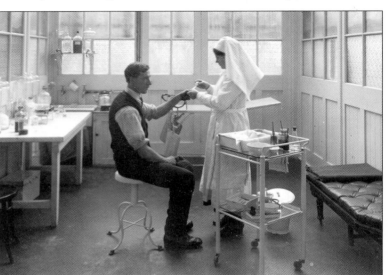

development made possible an almost endless list of new ideas: radio, radar, television, satellite communications, fax machines, radio astronomy, mobile phones, the internet and the ability to interconnect with and exchange information between billions of devices world-wide. In the 21st century further advances promise to give schools and universities everywhere the ability to access the best educationalists in the world; to provide people instant access to specialist advice and to choose the best entertainment in the world at a time to suit themselves. And a significant percentage of commuting can be removed from major cities: geographic location will become irrelevant to the successful conduct of business. In short the world will continue to radically change and improve as a result of advances in information and communication technology.

A world-leader in this technology, Marconi of Coventry, traces its origins to 1916. It was in that year, in the midst of the first world war, that an existing business

This page: *More scenes from the factory in the early 1920s.*

was bought by a Mr Gill. In fact Gill was a director of the Peel-Connor telephone company based at Adelphi in Salford, but he purchased the firm under his own name in order to keep the asking price down.

The Peel-Connor telephone works was soon established in Telephone Road, Stoke. At that time the factory manufactured electrical magnetos; the factory buildings comprised a boiler house, a foundry, material stores, a tool room, machine shop and an inspection and test assembly. The only drawback to the site was that the nearest railway siding was at Gosford Green.

Despite the post war recession demand for telephones would continue to grow and with it the Peel-Connor works with demand for telephones and switchboard gear ever rising. The factory expanding to include milling shops, millwrighting, woodworking, ebonite moulding, coil winding and cord braiding shops amongst many other departments.

Under the subsequent ownership of the General Electrical Co. Ltd, the Peel-Connor telephone business would acquire additional factories between the wars: after 1936 Whitefriars would be acquired shortly followed by Ford Street along with Triumph No 1 and No 2 together with the Queen Victoria Road branch and Spon Street, purchased at the outset of the second world war.

During the second world war part of the Coventry works was moved to Bradford where it would remain until 1947.

To Coventry residents the reason for such a move hardly needs explaining. The Coventry Wiring Shop and its on-site sewerage plant were bombed early in the war; whilst Whitefriars, Triumph No 1 and No 2 were all destroyed in 1940. To make up lost production between 1941 and 1945 a small factory was rented in

Leicester known as the Ashford Road Works and in 1942 premises were also occupied in Maryport until the war's end.

Despite the trials of war the company survived. Today Marconi supplies systems and infrastructure for information and communications networks operated by major operators such as BT and Cable & Wireless and by newer operators such as Energis and Colt as well as by large private businesses. The upgrading of existing networks to high speed broadband capability and increasing the speed of the internet are major areas of Marconi's capability.

In addition to supplying hardware to customers who have their own expertise to design and run networks the Marconi company can also provide customers with any necessary skills needed to plan, build and operate complete networks. And as well as communications and information systems the company is also strong in data and commerce systems.

Top: *A view of the factory at the start of the 21st century.*
Above: *An exterior view of the factory.*

and more efficient; they enable operators to offer lower and more flexible charges as well as many new applications and services.

The company works with its many different types of customers to analyse their current businesses and proposes ways in which their communications systems can be upgraded, improved and made more efficient. By working in partnership arrangements with customers Marconi can offer much more than competitive suppliers who simply offer products or services.

Not surprisingly the company aims to be the best information communications company in the world. Despite competition from such firms as Nortlel Networks in Canada, Lucent in the USA and Alcatel in France, Marconi believes that it can be the best by understanding and providing systems and expertise that will radically improve customers' networks and in turn their business and profitability.

And what's the next thing in telecommunications? Who can say; but if the next hundred years match the last then our great-grandchildren are going to be mightily impressed.

Marconi has supplied its systems to over 100 countries. It has a major presence in the USA, the UK, Germany, Italy and China. The same services are offered on a world wide basis but different countries act as 'centres of excellence' for specific company capabilities. For example the USA has expertise in high speed network access and internet systems, Italy has expertise in mobile systems for emergency services and the UK specialises in ultra high speed 'photonics transmission infrastructure' - optical fibre cable networks.

Most of the world's blue chip telecoms operators, whether long established or newer entrants buy systems and expertise from Marconi. In addition a large number of Internet Service Providers and large private businesses use Marconi systems. Marconi products make networks faster

Top left: *An aerial view of the site taken in 2000.*
Above left: *An interior view of the site.*
Below: *An exterior view of the site.*

Flying high

Dunlop is a name recognised throughout the world. It has been associated with many of the major developments in transportation for over a century. Today's Dunlop Aviation is based in Coventry and specialises in the design and manufacture of the wheels, brakes and braking systems for aircraft operated by airlines and airforces around the world.

From the earliest days of flying, aviation has made an increasing demand on wheels and brakes. As aircraft development became bigger and faster, higher landing speeds and heavier payloads have demanded even greater performance from the wheels, brakes and braking systems. Dunlop Aviation has led the way in meeting the challenge in these increased demands with major innovations such as carbon brakes and state-of-the-art braking systems. Dunlop Aviation has also been at the forefront of other technologies, including advanced composite materials and electro-thermal ice protection systems. ThrustSSC, the car which set the official supersonic record with a top speed of 763.035 mph, was fitted with wheels and brakes designed and made by Dunlop Aviation in Coventry.

Dunlop Aviation can trace its origins back to 1910 when the Dunlop Company produced its first catalogue of products aimed at the then fledgling aircraft industry. These products where little more than tyres and wire-spoke wheels, which had been adapted from contemporary cycle design practice.

The Dunlop Company dates back still further, to 1889, when John Boyd Dunlop and business partners joined

Top left: John Boyd Dunlop, 1840-1921. **Above right:** *First company brochure listing parts for aircraft, 1910.* **Below:** *The Blackburn Mercury of 1912, used Dunlop wheels and tyres. The design of the wire-spoke wheels obviously owes much to cycle rim technology*

William Thomson, who in the early 1840s had the idea of fitting air-filled tyres to horse-drawn carriages. Thomson's idea, which was not very practical, did not find favour so it was left to Dunlop, in 1888 to demonstrate the first practical pneumatic tyre.

Dunlop's development work was reportedly carried out on his son's tricycle and having perfected the idea he fitted pneumatic tyres to a bicycle that was entered in a race at Belfast Queen's College Sports. So impressive was the performance of this bike, compared with its solid tyre contemporaries that Dunlop's tyre became an overnight success and a transport revolution had begun.

In November 1889 John Boyd, Harvey du Cros and others entered into a partnership to form the Pneumatic Tyre Company and Booth's Cycle Agency Ltd. The company's factory was in Dublin but this did not meet with the approval of the local residents who objected to the unpleasant smells associated with tyre manufacture and a combination of pressure from the local council and lack of space to expand resulted in a decision to leave Ireland.

forces to exploit the recently developed pneumatic tyre. Given the achievements of the company throughout its history it will come as no surprise to learn that its founder was himself a remarkable man. Born in the Ayrshire village of Dreghorn in 1840 to a farming family, John Boyd Dunlop developed a love for animals. The quickness of his intellect and scope of his ability may be deduced from the fact that he graduated from Edinburgh Veterinary College as a qualified veterinary surgeon at the age of only 19 and in a short time had an extremely successful practice in the Belfast area of Northern Ireland.

It is often claimed that John Boyd Dunlop invented the pneumatic tyre, but this is not strictly true. True claim to this achievement rests with another Scot, Robert

At the end of the 19th century the bicycle was at the height of its popularity and the companies making these machines provided the principal outlet for the products of The Pneumatic Tyre Company. The City of Coventry was at the heart of the bicycle manufacturing industry and it was to this city that Dunlop moved his company when seeking a new home. Accordingly, in 1890, the company, apparently now trading as the Dunlop Pneumatic Tyre Company, moved into premises bounded by Alma Street and Raglan Street in Coventry. Thus started an association between community and company that has been

Top left: Beardmore Inflexible, 1928.
Above: Dunlop Rim and Wheel Company factory frontage, Holbrook Lane, 1940s. Right: An early exhibition showing a wide range of aviation wheels. On the left is the Beardmore Inflexible wheel of 1928, and third from left is the wire-spoke wheel for the De Havilland DH 66, 1927.

unbroken for over a century and one that has probably greatly assisted Coventry in attaining its position at the forefront of automobile development.

Working conditions at the Alma Street factory during the period just prior to the First World War required attendance from 6.00 am to 6.00 pm Mondays to Fridays plus 6.00 am to 1.00 pm on Saturdays. There were unpaid breaks for breakfast and lunch. Rates of pay were 6d (2.5p) per hour for skilled workers and 4 1/2d (just under 2p) per hour for the unskilled. At Christmas, Easter and Whitsuntide the factory closed for two days and in August there was a one-week holiday without pay.

Around 1904 tyre production was transferred to Aston, Birmingham where it remained for twelve years before moving again to the well known Fort Dunlop site in nearby Erdington.

Before any of these moves however the Alma Street factory began to diversify and in addition to cycle tyres was also

Above: An aerial view of the site taken in 1928. Holbrook Lane is across the bottom right hand corner with Munition Workers' hostels in the foreground. Foleshill Park can be seen in the middle distance.

making the rims and wheels. In 1908 Dunlop acquired the business and premises of the Stevenson Wheel Company Ltd of Wellington Street, Coventry, being renamed as the Dunlop Rim and Wheel Company Ltd.

The history of Dunlop's company would also be very different but for the existence of another well-established Coventry company, White & Poppe. They were pioneers in the production of the internal combustion engine and at various times their engines were used to power Ariel motor cycles, motor cars made by Singer and Morris and narrow-gauge locomotives. Their principal customer, however was Dennis Brothers of Guildford, makers of cars, lorries, buses and most famously, fire engines.

The onset of war in 1914 brought many changes at the Dunlop factories. Shortages of manpower meant that women became a familiar sight in the workplace and demand for wheels of all sizes soared. During the war period the demand for cycle rims had continued and Dunlop had found new applications for its wheel technology in the rapidly expanding automobile markets and the fledgling aircraft industry. As early as 1910 Dunlop had published a catalogue and price list containing details of tyres for aircraft and the Blackburn 'Mercury' of 1912 was fitted with the company's wheels and tyres that closely resembled products for the cycle industry. The price for a 24" x 3" tyre was £5 6s 0d per pair of tyres, £1 8s 9d per cover each and £1 4s 1d per tube each.

At the conclusion of hostilities in 1918, the Dunlop Rim and Wheel Company found itself in premises that restricted its future plans. The Armistice also had a profound effect on White & Poppe who had been heavily involved in munitions manufacture during the war. In 1919 the Dennis Bothers bought White & Poppe's engine and carburettor business and production was moved to Guildford. Arrangements were concluded for Dunlop to transfer to parts of the former munitions factory in Holbrooks and the move took place in 1919. This move established Dunlop on a site which some eighty years later it still occupies.

In 1925, in recognition of the growing importance of the aeroplane in early 20th century life, the Dunlop Board formed a separate Aviation Department with Joe Wright as manager. The company's early aircraft wheels had wire spokes and most

Right: A second world war spotter post.
Below: The Dunlop second world war emergency services, photographed just inside the Holbrook Lane gate.

aeroplanes had a fixed undercarriage, with the tail being supported by a skid, which also acted as a brake. At the time Dunlop was the principal supplier of cycle rims in the UK, with a company called Palmer holding the same position for aircraft. Sir Eric Geddes, Dunlop's chairman was also chairman of the fledgling Imperial Airways (later to become BOAC and ultimately British Airways) and Joe Wright lobbied him to specify Dunlop to supply wheels for the new aeroplanes instead of Palmer. This resulted in Imperial Airways new plane, the 14-seat De Havilland DH66 Hercules entering service in 1927 with Dunlop tyres and wheels, probably the last large British Commercial aircraft to be fitted with wire-spoke wheels.

The following year the Glasgow based firm, Beardmore and Company Ltd produced a new giant bomber for

the RAF. It was named "Inflexible", had three engines and a wingspan of 157 ft (48m) and was, at the time, the largest all metal monoplane to have flown successfully. Dunlop designed and manufactured the wheels that were 6 ft (1.8m) in diameter and had a steel rim supported by a centre section of light-alloy (aluminium) discs resulting in a significant weight saving without compromising strength. Two Beardmore Inflexible wheels are on public display, one at the Air Museum. Baginton and the other at the Science Museum, South Kensington.

As the size and weight of aircraft grew so did the need for reliable and controllable braking. In 1932 Dunlop produced a pneumatic brake for the Avro Avion aircraft. This was based on road vehicles' drum brakes; a steel drum containing a rubber air bag and a ring of brake pads was attached to the inside of the wheel hub. A re-chargeable air bottle would provide pressure to inflate the air bag which in turn would cause the brake pads to press against the inner diameter of the drum. The pilot would apply the brakes with a lever attached to his control stick, which also connected to the rudder controls, providing differential brake pressure for ground steering.

Preparations for conflict had started early at Holbrook Lane and in 1937 the Aviation department was training its workers in air-raid precautions. The evening of Thursday 14th November 1940 was cold, frosty and illuminated by a brilliant moonlight that enabled the Dunlop nightshift to pick their way through the blackout a little more easily than usual. As they made their way to work little did they realise that this was the night that Goering had chosen for his attempt to blitz Coventry out of existence. During the subsequent raid, the Dunlop site received thirteen direct hits by high explosive bombs and a number of others from incendiary devices. None of the nightshift was seriously injured although there were a few cases of shock. No substantial damage was caused. On the other side of Holbrook Lane an incendiary bomb hit the Brookville cinema and 'Gone with the Wind' was the last film to be shown there.

With the new breed of fast, highly manoeuvrable fighter planes, their pilots demanded faster weapons, as previously guns were fired using a trigger attached to the gun via a Bowden cable (not dissimilar to a bicycle brake cable) which caused a delay between a pilot pressing the trigger and the gun actually firing. Dunlop's designers led by Henry Trevaskis came up with a solution by using compressed air to fire the gun. This was activated by a small button in the pilot's joystick and its supremacy was proved in a gunnery contest. This resulted in the Dunlop firing mechanism being standard on all the RAF's new fighters such as Hurricanes and Spitfires and all the British fighters that took part in the "Battle of Britain". Later in the war the Americans developed an even more responsive and accurate all-electric gun firing system, but it proved too heavy and used too much

*Top right: De Havilland Dove owned and operated by Dunlop Aviation Division, 1950-57. **Above left:** Dunlop road fleet photographed in front of the Dunlop water tower. This tower rivalled Courtauld's chimneys and the gas holder as features of the north Coventry skyline. **Left:** Standing second from the left is Joe Wright, Manager of Dunlop Aviation.*

electrical power so Dunlop developed the idea into a more practical device. Shortly after the end of the war Dunlop were able to claim that "Every enemy plane destroyed by a British Fighter is shot down with the help of **Dunlop Gun-firing Gear**".

From the end of World War Two, for a period of about twenty years, Dunlop operated a number of aircraft, some for research work and others for transport purposes. This was an exciting time for aircraft development and Dunlop provided a number of important products which contributed to the progress in innovation and quality of the aircraft produced.

Aircraft brakes were constantly being updated and high pressure hydraulics would replace pneumatic systems and drum brakes. The Holbrook Lane designers turned their attention to disc brakes for the new generation of civil aircraft. These developed from brakes containing a single copper disc to multi-disc designs, with copper being replaced by steel and complete discs being replaced by segmented discs to minimise the distortion associated with the high temperatures experienced by aircraft brakes. The Vicker Viscount, which entered service in 1952 was fitted with Dunlop's multi-plate hydraulic brakes. As brake efficiency increased it occasionally resulted in the wheels locking and causing skid; rapid tyre wear would ensue and at worst tyres would burst causing a loss in directional control of the plane. An American company had designed a device that could detect the onset of wheel lock and would reduce the pressure at the brakes, preventing skidding and the British Government wanted Dunlop to manufacture the device under licence in the UK. Dunlop's Technical Director, Henry Trevaskis, was convinced he could improve the idea and developed his own solution; a practical, hydromechanical device evolved and was given the trade name "Maxaret". It proved so successful that the term Maxaret was used to describe any device that prevented wheel skids.

In the early 1950s Dunlop expanded into the premises vacated by Jaguar and were also invited to apply their brake technology to Jaguar's road racing cars. The Jaguar cars taking part in the 1953 Le Mans 24-Hour race were fitted with Dunlop disc brakes and finished first, second and fourth. This performance led to disc brakes being applied to nearly all road vehicles. With further development in aircraft technology and the increase in weight and size of planes and take-off and landing speeds, so wheels had to be bigger to cope with the larger brakes. Dunlop, under pressure from aircraft

manufacturers to keep weight to a minimum, developed carbon fibre to make their discs. After much testing this new material proved highly successful and when Concorde entered service in 1976 it was the first passenger aircraft in the world to be fitted with carbon brakes. This soon caught the attention of aircraft constructors on the other side of the Atlantic and within a few years Dunlop wheels and brakes were being fitted to the Boeing 757 passenger jet and the McDonnell-Douglas AV8B.

More recently, Dunlop wheels, carbon brakes, brake control and skid prevention systems have been fitted to the Dornier 328-300, a regional jet assembled in Germany, and the Typhoon (EFA); a European collaborative combat aircraft to replace the Tornado. The hydro-mechanical Maxaret has been replaced by an electronic "black box" and in the not too distant future brakes look set to become electronically operated rather than hydraulically.

Holbrook Lane has undergone many changes and survived the uncertainties of the economic climate of the 1980s and 90s. At the start of the 21st century Dunlop Aviation is a secure business serving the demanding needs of the international airspace industry while still relying on the dedication and tenacity of the people of Coventry who make up much of it's 800 workforce. The company looks forward with relish to the challenges, excitement and innovation that the new century holds.

Above: The poster issued following the second world war celebrating Dunlop's role in the "Battle of Britain".
Below: The Mori Seiki MT 4000, 21st century technology comes to Dunlop.

Powering the engines of success

'You got to have dream, if you don't have a dream - how you goin' to have a dream come true? asks the song from the musical, 'South Pacific'. The existence of the successful business Power Torque Engineering, which supplies markets throughout the world from its Binley base, can trace its origins back to the dream, considered completely unrealisable by many, of two brothers who came to Coventry in 1923 with the intention of selling Ford cars. Many considered their ambition quite mad and predicted they would be leaving the city after a few weeks, wiser but disillusioned men. However, the brothers, Fred and Frank Varney believed in Ford cars and were prepared to do everything necessary to sell them. They worked very hard but their efforts were rewarded and sales began to grow.

Their firm, Rugby Autocar, was established in 1920 when the brothers opened their first garage in Albert Street, Rugby. They had very little capital but a great deal of enthusiasm and they saw great possibilities for the future - how right they were. They worked seven days a week but their hard work eventually paid off. They attributed their success in their field to nothing but hard work and persistence, in sticking to it all the time and in never being satisfied with

Right: *Used car depot at the Old Mill, Wheatley Street.* **Below:** *The gateway to success.*

what they achieved. Also by concentrating only on products of one manufacturer, they were able to give the best possible service to all their customers.

By 1923 they had done so well that they decided to open in Coventry despite warnings given by their friends. They took premises in Bishop Street and tried to break into the Coventry car market. Frank is on record as saying, 'we came into Coventry, the lion's den, and feared neither machine nor man. We had faith in 'T' model Ford and the square engine and it held us in good stead.' The firm still possesses one of these early models and it has had airings over the years on special occasions from time to time, serving as elegant if rather

draughty transport for weddings. It also took part in the Ford centenary rally from London to Brighton in 1964.

A major contributing factor to their success was the first Ford small car, an 8hp model. Because of its compact size this model avoided the heavy tax duties and this put the Varneys slowly but surely on the road to success. The car trade was very different in those early days. Quite often someone purchasing a car would arrive by horse and cart. And there was no driving test then either.

Such was their success that by 1938 they had outgrown their Bishop Street site and moved to Pickford Brook, Allesley. During the Second

*Top: Showroom at Queen Victoria Road (at the end of the Arcade) Coventry. **Above:** Pan aerial view of the Rugby Autocar Co in the early 1960s. **Right:** 1922 one ton Model T Truck and a Norton NS2 Motorcycle used for PR purposes. Pictured at the Nuneaton Depot.*

World War the car market slumped but immediately afterwards the brothers found their feet again, and by 1949 were able to build a new garage at Rugby. About the same time another garage was built at Hinckley Road, Nuneaton, a venture which received recognition by being opened by Sir Patrick Hennessey, chairman of the Ford Motor Company.

In 1960 the family bought the Mill premises in Coventry's Wheatley Street and opened a second-hand car depot as well as a sizeable spares department. The following year the 'Motor Mart' on Walsgrave Road was taken over by the Rugby Autocar Company and opened as a showroom and service station. In the mid-1960s Rugby Autocar were advertising a second-hand 1961 Ford Anglia de-luxe, blue for £425 (£85 deposit) or 36 monthly payments of £11 19s 11d.

The years following the end of the Second World War saw a massive increase in car ownership and as cars became more plentiful, there developed a growing trade in second-hand cars and the Varneys opened a second-hand car depot in Rugby in 1962. They also went into the commercial vehicles side of the business and sold vans and Fordson tractors which soon became a large part of the total sales.

In 1963 Rugby Autocar Company opened their impressive new showrooms in Queen Victoria Road, Coventry which completed the development of the Queen Victoria Road section of the City Arcade. This replaced their existing showroom further down the road which was due to disappear during the central area redevelopment.

Commenting on problems the firm has experienced on the way to its present day success, the owners feel that they are 'too numerous to mention' - whatever the problems were they have obviously been largely overcome, and the experience has not deterred other

family members from taking on equal challenges in the same field as now there are members of the third generation of Varneys involved in the business.

It was natural that Fred's son, John was attracted to making his own contribution to his father's line of business and in 1969 he, together with Doug Hickson, founded Power Torque, based at the Allesley site dealing in industrial engines and components on behalf of Ford. They take pride in their ability to understand their client's requirements and

*Top: The Allesley Depot in the 1960s, the birthplace of Power Torque. **Above:** John Varney (centre), Andrew Varney (left), David Varney (right) at the 25th Anniversary of Power Torque becoming a Limited Company. **Left:** John Varney handing over the 50,000th engine supplied by Power Torque to Thwaites Engineering of Leamington Spa.*

provide cost effective solutions to their needs while supporting the future development of the client's business. They aim to provide a world-class service.

Power Torque supplies Ford power products to sports car manufacturers, special vehicle manufacturers, off-road machinery builders, generator set builders and vehicle fleets. By the end of 1976 they had sold over 50,000 engines and celebrated by holding a 'Ford Power on Show Exhibition' at Pickford Brook, Allesley.

They offer a huge range of engines and gearboxes and axles and there is almost certainly one appropriate for just about any application whether it be for special cars, taxis or tractors. They also have facilities for the servicing of the Ford content of machines made up of a variety of components. They undertake this work either in their own workshops or even on site. A range of reconditioned engines is also available.

In 1990 they moved into a new headquarters costing £1.5m in Herald Way, Binley. Performing the opening ceremony Ken Prendergast, executive director of customer services operations for Ford of Europe announced that based on the past performance of the company and all the potential for the future, Power Torque was the biggest Ford power product dealer in the world.

In the same way that Fred and Frank were able to see the potential of the car and its implications for the future, so John Varney also could see that the importance of the petrol fired engine will perhaps be considerably less in the future than it is today and he decided to invest in building up expertise in the development of alternative fuels. They began by working jointly with Perkins of Shrewsbury, the former Rolls-Royce diesel engine company, to produce gas-powered versions of their big engines and since then they have continued along this track and now they have over twenty years experience as market leaders in the development and conversion of engines for running on natural gas, biogases and LPG. This continues to be a growth area and as recently as 1999, four new employees were recruited to deal with this side of the business, including three vehicle technicians.

On the occasion of the opening of the new premises, John was presented with a special plaque to mark 40 years with the Rugby Autocar Group, the parent company.

They recently supplied the first LPG powered vehicles for Trafford Metropolitan Borough Council for duties as varied as drain maintenance and library deliveries. a total of 26

*Above: The famous flying car from the film Chitty Chitty Bang Bang. **Below:** Power Torque Engineering's new premises in the 1990.*

Transit, Escort and Courier vans were fitted with the Prins LPG system. This is likely to be the first of many such commissions as transport authorities are able to claim up to 75 per cent of the cost of converting vehicles to run on LPG from the Government under the Energy Saving Trust Scheme, which was set up to encourage the reduction of vehicle exhaust emissions.

One of Power Torque's leading Prins LPG technology dealers recently converted the famous Chitty Chitty Bang Bang to LPG. Chitty was the first James Bond style car required to race, fly and cross water.

Fitted with a Ford 3 litre V6 engine in 1968, the car was originally built for racing in 1920 with a Maybach Zeppelin engine.

Apart from 'own brand' gas engines, they have also carried out extensive research and development for major manufacturers, ultimately carrying out production conversion on their behalf. Many of these are in use on energy saving equipment and utilise the heat from the cooling and exhaust systems.

Such is the scale of the expertise the company has built up that they are not restricted to supplying off-the-shelf equipment manufactured by Ford but are able to call on the skill of drawing office and design staff and are able to help tailor the unit to fit directly into the client's equipment, thus easing production and lowering costs. Dynamometers capable of handling up to 600kW, exhaust analysers and other test facilities are also available.

Power Torque stocks a wide range of diesel and gas engines for virtually all applications from forklift trucks to narrow boats. They hold franchises to supply Ford, Iveco, New Holland and Lombardina diesel engines. These conform to all current European and US requirements and are constantly updated and improved to keep them abreast of changes in legislation.

The company supplies Ford engines and components to firms such as Morgan, Lti and JCB as well as standby generators for hospitals and public buildings, and engines and compressors for boats. In fact Morgan is one of their oldest customers. They began fitting Ford engines as long ago as 1934. They recently produced a new 4x4 four seater car, featuring comfortable rear seats with Mondeo catches and the MVH 418 engine. The new century began with important changes in the personnel of Power Torque. Two grandsons of

Top: Ford on show - open day at the Allesley Works.
Left: Assembly of one of the specialised powertrains supplied by Power Torque.

Fred Varney have been appointed to two key positions in the firm. Andrew Varney took over the Managing Director role and his cousin David took over as Deputy Managing Director. They also said farewell to Brian Pitchford who had given 41 years continuous service to the company. David Vickers, Special Director of Sales scooped the Salesman of the Year award from Ford Power products recently. The company has grown considerably over the years and now has 47 members of staff in workshop, stores, sales and administration, contributing to the local economy by providing Coventry people with employment.

David Varney represented the firm recently at Buckingham Palace when, along with a representative from Metrocab, he handed over the latest LPG Metrocab for the exclusive use of a member of the Royal Family. The cab is powered by the Ford DOC420 Spark ignition engine which gives good exhaust emissions performance.

The firm carries a large stock in its Parts Department, enabling quick sourcing of equipment and parts for servicing. It is manned by staff who are involved in the supply of original equipment and are therefore able to recognise the lesser known and specialist parts fitted to some machines. In short, they know about engines and engineering.

Power Torque have supplied engines to most parts of the world for a variety of applications. From heating in Holland to cooling in Canada, trucks in Turkey to vehicles in Venezuela.

In 1999 they were selected by Lombardini to provide sales and service support wherever required. This is a great opportunity for them to build on their already extensive experience and enlarge their range of diesel and spark ignition engines.

With such an impressive history of service and achievement going back around ninety years and extending over the working lives of three generations of the Varney family there is undoubtedly a bright future for the business. One advantage of the family run business is that good relationships can be built up with customers who after receiving good service will come back again and again. No-one believes future success will be achieved without effort, the same philosophy of hard work and seeking to provide the customer with his requirements to deadline and budget will still be needed, but the company is certainly looking forward to what lies ahead. Building on past success, without complacency, Power Torque plans to broaden its customer base and invest in obtaining new markets, continually striving to consolidate the business. They hope that many firms and individuals will continue to Talk Power to Power Torque.

Top: Andrew Varney explaining the operation of an LPG vehicle to HRH The Duke of Edinburgh at the Royal Mews. Above left: David Varney, Deputy MD. Right: Andrew Varney, MD.

Pressing changes

How many of us know what goes on under the bonnet of our cars? These days engines seem so complicated we are no longer quite as sure as we were in our youths exactly which bit is which. But there are some parts we still recognise: spark plugs, timing belt and the radiator - even if more often than not the radiator is now hidden behind the housing for an electric fan.

What we usually think of as 'the engine' is really a collection of many special parts surrounding the engine itself and all jumbled together under the bonnet. Car manufacturers do not make all those parts themselves, no matter what the more innocent car owner may believe. Those who live in the Midlands are well aware that car makers are mainly component assemblers buying in most of the thousands of parts they need to put together to

make the vehicles they sell. But who manufactures all those pieces - and in particular who makes all those millions of radiators?

Those who are unfamiliar with the world of engineering might be forgiven for assuming that a firm which has the word 'pressworks' in its title has some connection with the printing trade. But not so; the local firm Sofedit UK which has until recently been known as Coventry Presswork has been involved in making metal parts for the car industry for more than a century.

The foundations of the Coventry Radiator & Presswork Company Limited were laid during the last part of the 19th century and the company therefore played a major part in the

Above: One of the company's earliest factories.
Right: An early company radiator in a Humber.

development of the automotive industry during its formative years, a hard testing period of sustained technical progress and rapid expansion.

The firm's founders were the Jackson family. Their business began in 1890 when two Jackson bothers, who had originally been in business as scrap metal collectors, began making metal parts such as washers from the scrap they collected. They worked from premises in Trafalgar Street; the firm's present Canley site being occupied from the 1930s.

It was however not until 1912 that the firm known as Coventry Radiator or CovRad properly began. The sons of the two Jackson brothers would in turn eventually join the business, which would remain under Jackson family management for two generations.

Like most large companies the firm had begun modestly enough, but it quickly established a reputation for its high quality products. The ensuing years brought increasing demands from the growing motor industry for radiators, presswork, plated parts and many other components.

Very few motor vehicles were on the roads when the Jackson brothers had begun their small business. The roads of Britain were still filled with trams, steam driven vehicles and electric cars and millions more horses were still pulling carriages, drays and cabs. Who then would have guessed at the explosive increase in the number of vehicles which would soon come to dominate our roads? Even though there may not have been today's millions of cars there were however still thousands on the roads, and supplying their manufacturers would become a steady market for the Jackson brothers. That market would soon show a sharp increase as the demands of the military for motorised transport to supplement its horse-drawn transport during the first world war of 1914-18 would provide the incentive for manufacturers across Britain, and especially in Coventry, to meet that need.

The next two decades would not prove as daunting to the car industry as others. The brief lived post war boom of the roaring twenties would not last long. Whilst it did people bought cars. And when the bubble did burst and the great depression of the 1930s hit, people still bought cars. The motor car was a thing of its time and recession or not the public still bought more each year than the year before. In 1930, to meet those burgeoning, demands a new factory was built and equipped at Burnsall Road, Canley which

Top: *A line-up of company delivery vehicles from the 1950s.* **Above:** *A Rolls Royce radiator.* **Right:** *A craftsman in the Tool & Die Shop.*

would eventually develop into today's modern plant.

During the second world war the company made parts for Spitfires and tank radiators. The factory was also used to make ammunition, and it naturally became a target for enemy bombers.

For many years the activities of the company extended into other fields of industry apart from the motor trade. The post war years saw massive increases in demand. Press Shop no 3 was constructed in 1954 and no 4 Press Shop in 1962. The completion of that new press shop in the 1960s, one of the finest in the country, would greatly increase the firm's capacity to produce a wide range of products.

In the late 1950s the company had decided to build the entirely new shop designed specifically for the competitive

high speed production of presswork. The new shop would incorporate all the most recent developments in the field, heavy presses being mounted on a steel grillage system over a basement area, allowing maximum flexibility of layout for subsequent alterations and expansion. Smaller presses were converted into mobile units which could be easily moved into position by heavy-duty overhead cranes for each production run.

A steel store would run the entire length of the building alongside the presses, containing equipment for automatic cutting-off of stock from coils and sheets and allowing direct feeding to each group of presses.

The most modern presses would be installed and the ancillary equipment would include monorail conveyor systems, mobile interpress conveyors and underground scrap disposal conveyors incorporating a fully automatic hydraulic bailing plant.

Careful planning had ensured flow-line production wherever possible and the greatest use would be made of mechanical ejection devices for speeding the movement of components between presses. Mezzanine floors would run the entire length of both sides of the shop and accommodate additional fabrication and subsidiary processes. The galleries were supplied direct from the presses by the monorail conveyer system. The sub-assembly sections were also planned for flow-line production and the

Right: Polishing a radiator.
Below: Engineering draughtsmen in the design department.

handling of work was therefore reduced to a minimum.

The new presses would range from 40 to 700 tons capacity and produce an extraordinary variety of products for almost every branch of industry.

Those new presses would incorporate all the latest design features including totally enclosed electrical wiring and equipment and air piping. Controls were arranged for the greatest flexibility of operation and in-built rotary cam units would permit the use of up to eight separate automatic operations during each stroke of the press.

Main services and control gear would be located in the basement enabling maintenance to be carried out with minimal interference to production.

Adjacent to the main works in Burnsall Road would be the firm's Service Department. The building was designed and erected for the specific purpose of repairing and reconditioning all types of radiators, whether made by the company or not, and would provide a major service to the whole motor trade.

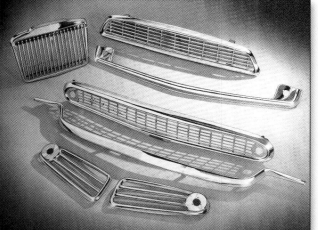

By now the company's name had become familiar to thousands of people outside Coventry. To ensure prompt delivery to customers the company maintained a large fleet of heavy trucks, pantechnicons, flat trailers and light vans, many specifically designed and constructed to transport the company's own products. The vehicles bearing the 'CovRad' name or the longer Coventry Radiator and Presswork Co. Ltd would be a common sight on Britain's roads.

For those who worked for the company working conditions had never been better. The business held its workers in high esteem and their welfare was a matter of paramount importance. The canteen adjacent to the works was of ultra-modern design with excellent facilities and all the latest equipment.

A new surgery had also been recently built and equipped with modern surgical apparatus. A fully qualified nurse was always in attendance during working hours and a doctor would be regularly available for consultation.

And the well organised company sports club had fields situated near the main works in an attractive setting along with football and cricket pitches, tennis courts and a bowling green.

Top: The plating department.
Above: The finished product.

The company had also been a pioneer of a contributory pension scheme applicable to all works and staff employees. This was of considerable importance when, due to the unusually low staff turnover, more than 10 per cent of the firm's employees could boast of more than 21 years service and become members of what had become known as the '21 Club'.

Within its new state of the art factory the company would not simply produce radiators; the range of products for the automotive industry would be almost endless: brake shoes, rocker covers, fans, petrol tanks, chrome grills and boot lids were just some of the many car parts being turned off the production line and being shipped in an endless stream to car assembly plants across the country.

Amongst its better known products outside the motor industry would be industrial oil and gas fired space heaters, condensers for refrigeration and air conditioning units, oil coolers and heat exchangers for internal combustion engines and for processing liquids in the chemical and oil industries.

Many British cars and most of the UK's commercial vehicles, tractors and stationary engines would be equipped with Coventry Radiators which was enjoying an international reputation.

In fact by the 1960s the company was the largest manufacturer of car radiators in the country and British cars fitted with Coventry Radiators and Presswork parts were to be found in every country in the world; amongst them would be Austin, Daimler, Armstrong Siddeley, Rootes, Standard and Triumph.

Commercial vehicles bearing famous names like AEC, Leyland, Thornycroft, Albion, Bristol, ERF, Guy, Scammel , Vickers and Foden would all be fitted with heavy duty radiators from Coventry. Similar radiators would also be fitted to stationary engines and power packs by firms such as Rolls-Royce, Consolidated Pneumatic Toll, Davy Paxman, Dorman, Murex, Holman and Perkins.

From 1965 name changes and take-overs would become part of the company's future: in that year the firm became Associated Engineering.

In the mid 1970s, despite a balance sheet showing eight million pounds worth of investment and annual sales of £17 million, demand for the products of what was by then Covrad Ltd appeared to be slowing. The company's 1,300 staff received a less than optimistic report from the managing director about the company's prospects unless everyone from top management to shop floor pulled their socks up.

Right: A small selection of vehicle components produced by the firm.
Below: The premises in the 1950s.

Ownership by Lebranchu would not however last long. In 1994 Coventry Presswork would become a subsidiary of another French business, the Paris based Sofedit SA company which itself was part of the multinational giant Trianon Industries Corporation.

On 1st April 2001 the company would acquire the new formal name of Sofedit UK Ltd. Sales remain primarily to car manufacturers such as Jaguar, Peugeot, Toyota and Vauxhall in the UK, and Renault and Mercedes abroad.

The firm's reputation today rests as much on quality, continuous improvement and the ability to deliver on time as it did in its earliest days when the Jackson brothers set out on a course which would see their small engineering firm grow to become one of the most important firms in a city noted for its many industrial titans.

To meet the challenges 'Covrad Pressworks' and Willenhall Manufacturing would combine their resources and technical expertise to offer an unrivalled presswork and assembly facility. Not only that, Covrad and WM would offer provide technical services to major companies in the vehicle, domestic appliances and electrical industries to help them develop their own new products.

Despite such enterprise more corporate battles and name changes would soon come about. By 1980 the Presswork side of Covrad had become Armstrong Equipment, and only five years later Armstrong Presswork. And just two years later again the firm would be known as Coventry Presswork - itself to become a wholly owned subsidiary of the Lebranchu group in 1991. The Lebranchu group of companies had been founded in 1925 as a manufacturer of prototypes for the French automobile industry. Lebranchu had begun the develop design and volume production facilities in the mid 1960s which had quite rapidly become the foundation of a much larger group.

The site at Coventry with its autonomous engineering, quality and commercial facilities covering some eight acres and containing 330,000 sq. ft of manufacturing space with a range of over 100 presses from 40 to 1500 tonnes including transfer, double action and blanking would be handy acquisition for Lebranchu.

So the next time you go poking under your car bonnet to top up the oil or add some windscreen washer fluid look at the various engine parts. The chances are that they have been made in Coventry by this long-lived local firm which has employed many thousands of the city's workers over its long history.

Top left: *21st century manufacturing.*
Below: *Coventry Presswork.*

Three generations of good hair days

Starting a business inevitably involves taking considerable risks, but to do so in 1930, soon after the commencement of a deep economic depression across the world, in the supply of hairdressing products (at that time, only the wealthy had the spare cash for hair-dos) involved far more than most. This, however is what one Birmingham couple did.

They started out in two small rooms in the basement of an office block in Navigation Street, Birmingham with £25 of borrowed money. The courageous couple were Ernest and Ethel Agnes Foxton but their company was named E A Ellison & Co Ltd as Miss Ellison was very well known in the trade before she became Mrs Foxton.

It was far from being an act of sheer folly, however, the depth of trade knowledge the Foxtons possessed and their proximity to company warehouses and wholesalers meant they were in a good position to meet a demand. They also had an innovative approach to business. At a time when it was unheard of for wholesalers to deliver to customers, Ellisons, as early as 1932, had an agreement with one of their customers, a Mr Harold Jeavons, to share the costs of running an Austin 7 Ruby Saloon. The arrangement worked quite

well for a time, Ellisons having it during the week and Mr Jeavons at weekends. Offering such a good service put the fledgling business well on the road to success, no one could beat them. However it wasn't long before this vehicle became too small for Ellisons' requirements and a larger vehicle was purchased for the Company's sole use.

Business would doubtlessly have gone from strength to strength from that point on, but Ellisons, in common with everyone else found their plans rudely interrupted by the second world war. Not only were valued staff members required for the war effort, but there was also the problem of rationing of supplies as well as petrol.

This was bad enough, but in December, 1940 the warehouse suffered when a land mine exploded and blew out all the windows, the ceilings came down and virtually all the stock was ruined. Premises opposite the Alexandra Theatre were hastily rented and all stock which could be salvaged was moved. It is said that a fur powder puff was lodged in overhead cables in a nearby street until June 1941, but this may be an exaggeration!

After the war, the enterprise and hard work of Leslie Bell, who had joined the company in 1934 at the tender age of 14 on wages of 8/- (40p) per week, steadily built up the business again. A new warehouse was required as the original one had a demolition order placed on it.

The 1960s were times of major changes; new ideas, new business practices and new business strategies took shape. Once again Ellisons scored a first when they opened up a Cash and Carry warehouse on Exhall Trading Estate, Coventry which was run by Jim

Above centre: 1948, Miss Ellison (the founder 1930) with Pam Heath to become joint MD with husband John in 1990. Left: Austin 7 Ruby saloon - the firm's first vehicle.

In the 1970s the High Street beauty salons were starting to appear and beauty treatments were becoming more accessible to ordinary people as opposed to only the rich and famous. John Heath and his wife Pam took an interest in this part of the business and added carefully selected beauty products to the existing Ellison ranges. This was an area of rapid growth, and now Ellisons is the main supplier to the beauty industry. They supply Hairdressing Salons , Beauty Salons , Health Spas, Training Colleges, Hotel and Leisure Groups, Cruise Liners, Nail Studios and Aromatherapists as well as ex-pats who set up beauty salons in various parts of the world. Much of this business comes from personal word-of-mouth recommendation.

In the early days Ellisons experienced great difficulty with deliveries of shampoo. No two deliveries were alike in colour or consistency, and so in 1960 they started producing their own. This involved Leslie Bell taking the necessary materials home at the weekend, and with his wife Bren at the helm, the Bell family succeeded in making 100 gallons of shampoo over the two days. This became a very profitable venture and was soon expanded to the manufacture of other products, a

and Barbara Allworth. This was a considerable undertaking and when the warehouse opened all the items on sale had to be individually priced - thousands of items. Staff worked for several days displaying and pricing stock. However, the Chancellor of the Exchequer changed the rates of purchase tax in his Budget of that year, completely to everyone's surprise. It was then a case of getting all available hands on deck to reprice everything overnight. Friends and family were drafted in to work alongside staff around the clock to achieve this. They opened on time, even if they were feeling a little tired.

Top: 1938 Wolseley Motors Senior Staff; Working colleagues who never knew that their grandchildren would marry and successfully expand a small Birmingham based hairdressing supplier into a national business supplying professional hair and beauty salons. First left Joe Rowley - grandfather of John. Far right Jack Mitchell - grandfather of Pam. Top right: The first beauty catalogue in 1981, consisted of eight black and white pages. Above right: The 2001 Beauty Buyers guide with over 170 full colour pages. Above left: An early invoice dated 1965. Right: Colin Lewis, twice World Champion, the firm's first guest tutor.

methylated spirits tank was installed outside to enable lacquer to be made.

The firm inaugurated a Tuition Centre in their Leicester branch, to which top London stylists were invited to give workshop type tuition to small groups of hairdressers, and Sunday cutting and styling workshops became a regular feature. Another first for Ellisons with salon owners wishing to keep up to date with fashion no longer having to travel to London and pay high prices. Colin Lewis, twice World Champion Hairdresser was their first guest tutor.

By 1987 the Coventry Cash and Carry warehouse was becoming too small, and a luxury extension was built. Joshua Galvin, known as the 'hairdressers' hairdresser' and his team gave a fast moving demonstration of cutting, perming and colouring on 15 models. A wide variety of commercial work was shown. The design of the warehouse, as well as the provision of a large carpark, are all intended to make shopping there convenient and enjoyable.

They continue to keep up with, and anticipate trends. In the beauty sector they have many products that offer genuine benefits to beauty therapists and their clients. In hairdressing and beauty they start to build an impressive selection of branded products which continues to this day keeping their customers up-to-date in this fast moving business.

Above: Joshua Galvin and his team demonstrate their skills at the new cash and carry, 1987. **Below:** A staff picture, Mr and Mrs Heath are fourth and fifth from left on the back row. Pam Linforth, Director of Personnel is third from left on the back row and Sales Director, Laurence Green is standing far right.

haircutting scissors with a £200 price tag is a regular occurrence.

As well as top quality products, Ellisons is proud to have a dedicated and knowledgeable staff. There are professional beauty therapists on the management team and the entire sales team out on the road consists of qualified therapists. The Cash and Carry branches in Birmingham, Coventry and Leicester are staffed by well-trained and enthusiastic people.

No business can afford to rest on its past achievements and Directors are constantly reviewing the strategic development of the business to identify opportunities. The company has grown enormously over the years and now employs 150 people. Ellisons recently acquired a Dutch manufacturer of top quality hair and beauty salon furniture. With sales all across mainland Europe, this is an important development opening up many additional opportunities. On the hairdressing side of things, they have recently been appointed sole UK importer for some of the top brands of haircare products from the USA.

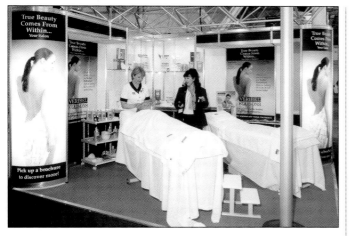

Top left: Pamela Linforth, far right and Sally Dick, centre with their Advanced electrolysis students.
Left: One of five Ellisons stands at a Trade Exhibition.
Below: Ellison's Coventry Headquarters.

Throughout all this change - the customer base and range of products is hugely greater than in the early years - the company philosophy remains the same. They seek to treat the customer as they themselves would wish to be treated. Ellison's integrity and reputation for fair dealing is known throughout the industry.

The product range they offer is incredibly diverse - everything from grips and pins, lotions and potions to furniture and electrical equipment. At Ellisons you can get everything you need to fully equip and stock a new hairdressing salon. Customers demand high quality products, and selling precision

Building a quality reputation

Many readers will be familiar with the name Benfield, a name which has been synonymous with construction in the Coventry area for many years. Yet it is not just houses that have been built, the range of business activities as well as the firm's reputation has also been built up in the years since Kenneth Bertram Benfield established the company in 1933.

At that time he operated from a shed in the back garden of his home in Whitefriars Street, Coventry. He was a time served carpenter and builder and worked as a jobbing builder undertaking carpentry work and property repairs including renewing sash cords on windows. He opened an account at the Midland Bank Ltd with £15 of his savings. One of his very first jobs was to make a pedestal writing desk. As no transport was available and he could not afford to buy a vehicle, he hired a greengrocer's cart for an hour for the sum of sixpence, in order that the completed desk could be delivered to an address in Grosvenor Road. On another occasion he pushed a wheelbarrow full of sand and cement from George Nicholls in Gosford Street to a house in Queen Street to fix a fireplace because he could not afford a handcart.

Business continued to develop by way of sash cords, garden gates, stopped drains and

broken windows, until in 1936 the firm's name was placed on the list of approved repairers for the Education Committee, within the scale of £1 to £20. In 1937 Ken was joined by Harold Brain who had been apprenticed at the same time and with the same firm,

who brought an injection of capital to the tune of £100 to the company. The company was registered under the name of K B Benfield & Co and the firm started undertaking small contract works for the Corporation up to the value of £1500. Both of the principals were competent in the matters of estimating and quantity surveying having completed the full building and surveying course at the Old Technical College in Earl Street while they were apprentices.

*Above Left: Company founder, Kenneth Benfield.
Above right: The firm's second lorry and driver Cyril Berry, opposite the yard on St John Street in the mid 1930s. Right and below: Air raid shelters constructed for the Coventry Corporation in 1940.*

Today the name Benfield is associated with a Group of seven companies, four of which are, Chartered Building Companies associated with quality and service in the areas of house building, building contracting, and property development and investment.

How different it was in the early days from now. For the first year, Kenneth Benfield was on his own, he kept his own accounts and did his own drawings and designs. He was soon able to employ another carpenter and in 1937 he took a tenancy on St John's Ambulance garage in St John Street, Coventry and subsequently rented land at the side of this. It was at this site he was able to take on joinery work for local builders. Business grew steadily and around 1945 he moved to offices and a hardware shop at Bell Green.

It is seldom easy for small businesses in the early years and Kenneth Benfield experienced his fair share of difficulties along the way, especially the problems

associated with clients who were slow at paying for work he had completed.

While the Benfields, along with all other families in Coventry, had numerous anxious moments in the second world war from the threat of bombing raids, it was a beneficial time for business as the firm was given a contract to build air-raid shelters. Other work was forthcoming and business expanded as a 'reserve occupation'.

Though the Benfield name is best known in the West Midlands, the firm has long-standing connections with areas much further afield. The company ventured into Malta in the 1960s. They built a housing estate, a school, the Kennedy Memorial all out of

Above: *Scenes of devastation on Little Park Street, Coventry in November 1940. Just around the corner from Benfield's yard.*

Below: *Benfields constructing the first Rocket factory for Rolls Royce at Ansty, near Coventry in 1954.*

joined the company in 1977 and took over general control of the house-building side, pushing production up to 100 houses per year. Clive, a Chartered Builder, is now Group Managing Director, but Ken Benfield still maintains an active involvement in all businesses as Group Chairman.

There is a long and honourable tradition of public service connected with the Benfield name. The firm was the driving force behind the drive to raise the necessary funds for the restoration of Coventry Cathedral Spire between 1976-79. In 1978 after many years service as a City Councillor and serving as Chairman of the Public Works and Public Health and Environment Committees, Ken Benfield was elected as the Right Worshipful The Lord Mayor of Coventry.

local stone. They also tendered for work in Libya but withdrew on the advice from the British Consulate there when Colonel Gadaffi came to power.

The firm is very much a family business. Having served his apprenticeship as a carpenter and builder and gained an Honours degree in Building, Ken's son, Clive

The size of the Benfield Group means that it can handle very large projects with ease. It was jointly responsible for the redevelopment of Tower Court on the Foleshill Enterprise Park, situated at the junction of Lockhurst Lane and Foleshill

*Top: Building the main pumping station at Ramsey in Cambridgeshire. **Above:** Constructing the tunnel under the river at Ramsey. **Right:** Celebrating as the two sides of the tunnel meet under the river.*

the House Builders' Federation. Clive Benfield has taken great interest in the activities of the construction industry and has served on various committees concerned with promoting excellence in the industry in the Midlands region over many years, and nationally as Chairman of the Construction Confederation, Chairman of the Chartered Building Company and Consultancy Board also numerous other positions including Chairman of the CITB Partnership Centre for Coventry and Warwickshire.

Benfield Homes have been pleased to work with the Construction Industry Partnership Centre over many years in arranging visits to building sites by school pupils and teachers so that they can see for themselves how houses are built, children can see the whole range of jobs involved right from digging the foundations to putting in the finishing touches of a co-ordinated colour scheme. They hope to foster an interest in the industry which will lead to youngsters considering choosing it as a career.

With such a background, it is very likely that Benfields will continue to build their reputation as well as houses for many years to come.

Road, approximately one mile north of Coventry city centre. The site was formerly occupied by the headquarters of Courtaulds plc. They are, however, equally at home working, whether in Coventry or further afield, on smaller projects and there are numerous other Benfield projects to be seen around the region, including schools, colleges, nursing homes, churches, industrial and commercial buildings and building work for housing associations and domestic clients.

Whatever the task in hand the same philosophy applies. The companies in the Benfield Group seek to provide a service which is second to none. Their goal is zero defects on handover and to provide their clients with cost effective, quality buildings whatever they may be, and to create a pleasant environment, combined with solid construction, low maintenance and affordable running costs.

Four of the Group companies are Chartered Building Companies which means that the client has the assurance that those who run the company are professional and qualified builders operating under a strict code of conduct and who are aware of their responsibilities towards health and safety and have a desire to provide their customers with a first class construction service every time. The group is also in membership of the National Federation of Builders and

*Top left: The interior of the Dove Public House, Leicester. Totally refurbished by the firm. **Above:** An artist's impression of Tower Court, a joint project undertaken by Deeley Properties and Benfield Group to refurbish the former Courtaulds head offices in Foleshill, Coventry. **Right:** Clive Benfield the Group Managing Director.*

Covering the World's floors

What have you got covering your kitchen floor? Ceramic tiles? Carpet? Polished wood?

The number of choices available to us today is bewildering, but many older residents of Coventry will recall the days when the choice was far more limited. They will remember days when no floor covering at all was still common and when cleaning the floor meant taking the furniture out into the yard and throwing buckets of water over the floor before brushing the water out of the door.

Often in the poorest homes the only floor covering you were likely to see was a rag rug in front of the coal fire; something to put one's feet on and which at least stopped the cold and damp seeping into your bones.

But not everyone was so badly off. Many of us had lino to cover our floors. Do you recall that stiff awkward stuff that seemed to crack so easily wherever it was laid over an uneven surface? Do you recall father coming home with a cheap roll of it tied with twine and hearing him suddenly using some choice 'shop floor' language when he cut his finger with his Stanley knife when he tried to fit the stuff round an awkward spot? In case you've forgotten lino was short for linoleum or 'linoleum' - oil cloth which had seen a boom in sales during its early history due to the campaign against TB. Lino was more hygienic than other flooring products in that it was easily wiped clean when TB carriers spat or coughed on the floor - oh happy days!

Top left: Company founder John Harris.
Right: The old packaging department in the late 1970s. Below: Production in the 1980s.

Back in 1977 however, twelve years after its formation, the company established its own distribution network in the UK

With the growth in the retail industry during the 1980s Amtico's business boomed - its floors could be found in nearly every major high street shop. The company began to develop new cutting methods and new ways of using high fidelity printing techniques to produce high quality reproductions of natural material.

With rapid growth in demand from the commercial market for its 'wood' products the company expanded its manufacturing facility in 1988 and built a second factory situated on the site of the old Jaguar plant in Kingfield Road, almost opposite the existing site.

In the 21st century however things have moved on: Coventry is home to Amtico, one of the world's leading manufacturers of floor coverings. The firm's astounding products would have left our parents and grandparents gasping with amazement at the stupendous quality and range of materials now available.

Amtico was set up in Coventry on the main Courtaulds site in 1965. The new business was a joint venture between Courtaulds and American Biltrite. Courtaulds' main activity in 1965 was acrylic yarn; the manufacture of vinyl (PVC) flooring was a diversification from that core business, but one which looked a promising venture.

By 1969 Courtaulds had acquired the whole business in the UK, and with it the licence to use the Amtico brand name in almost every country outside of North America.

John Harris was seconded to Amtico as a chemist and worked through every aspect of manufacturing before being put in charge of the company. That secondment would last far longer than he expected: John would remain to oversee the development and expansion of the company and its products beyond the millennium.

Top left: An aerial view of the premises in the 1970s.
Right: Company vehicles with the Amtico logo in the 1980s.

The Duke of Kent presiding over the official opening of the new factory in 1989 rightly hailed it as a new era for the company.

With the opening of the new factory a decision was taken to shift the ratio of commercial to residential business in the UK to 50-50. A process of rebranding and expanding the business began in earnest to increase sales to homeowners and house builders.

In 1989 the first Amtico Studio was opened in Epsom, Surrey which became a showcase for the company's products and encouraged the home owner to create their own flooring designs. The company also opened its first

overseas operation in Germany and formed Amtico International GmbH. Expansion continued with the opening of a Studio in Dusseldorf in Germany in 1991 and a Munich showroom the following year, along with another in Sheffield.

In 1991 the company revolutionised its manufacturing operations and introduced the Japanese 'just-in-time' manufacturing system - no large stocks of material would tie up valuable space, time and capital - orders were literally made just in time. That year the company also began to develop computerised CAD/CAM techniques - at that time unheard of in the flooring industry.

Using computers meant that Amtico floors could be made to customers' own designs and cut to order. Such developments would culminate in the firm's present ability to make it possible to despatch individual designs within just four days.

Over the next four years the company grew a global network of studios and set up yet another company in Australia. When

Top right: *Laboratory testing.*
Left: *A state-of-the art showroom.*
Below: *Factory production.*
Below right: *Product testing.*

in 1993 the business acquired the rights to use the Amtico name in North America studios in Atlanta and New York were opened in the USA and Amtico International Inc. was formed.

Around the same time the company also established the Amtico Approved Retailer scheme in the UK to support its growing residential business.

One of the most critical years in Amtico's history would come in 1995 when the company experienced a management buy-out from Courtaulds. Confidence in the company's future was well founded. Following the buy-out the business went on to see even greater success, more than doubling sales over the next five years.

No-one should have been too surprised: in the same year the firm had become the first hard flooring manufacturer to achieve Environmental Management Accreditation (ISO 14001) for its manufacturing processes, and the following year the company won the DTI's Best Small Business Award.

By 1997 the company was able to launch a product it had been developing in Coventry for some years - Stratica - a new type of resilient flooring which did not contain any plasticisers and one to which the British Design Council would eventually give Millennium Project status.

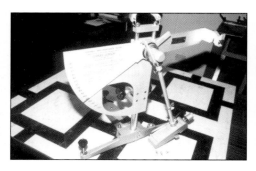

able to deliver what is requested. Cutting edge technology of the most literal kind ensures that the company can always 'make it happen' with its reputation for thriving on problem solving and tight deadlines and an international design team which can develop detailed computer drawings from customers' instructions to create exactly the floor they want, when the want it. 'If you can imagine it we can produce it' is the company's promise. Amtico pioneered the technology of cutting high-design floors. Today curves, special shapes, custom made patterns and even intricate typography can all be accommodated. Customers can introduce borders, motifs or even their own corporate logos into their chosen floor design. With Amtico anything really is possible.

It is no surprise to discover that the company's products are found not only in thousands of homes but also grace some of the most prestigious locations in the world. Amtico floors now feature in such important sites as the Te Papa Museum in New Zealand, the NBC studios in the USA, aboard Stena Line ships and the USA's World Trade Centre.

Quieter and warmer than natural materials none of Amtico's 250 products will warp, crack, chip or splinter, a far cry from the cracked broken floor coverings we remember from our childhood.

The company now aims to build on its strengths and skill base. Retaining its R&D and product development department on the Coventry site the company's philosophy - to become the most exciting flooring company in the world - still drives it forward in continuous product innovation and ever-improving manufacturing techniques.

Left, both pictures: Two examples of Amtico flooring designs. ***Top right:*** *The Duke of Kent with John Harris at the opening of the new factory in 1989.*
Below: *Amtico's headquarters in Coventry.*

The first factory outside Coventry was built in Madison Georgia in 1998 to facilitate the growing business in the USA and to support their businesses in Australia and the Far East. It would also relieve capacity constraints in the UK to allow for further expansion into Europe.

Since then the company established more businesses in Europe developing a French subsidiary in 1999 and one in Sweden in 2001 whilst opening its New York Design Studio in Summer of 2001.

Today Amtico's products are sold throughout the world and the company is acknowledged as the market leader in the luxury flooring industry.

Practicality, durability and total individuality set Amtico's floor coverings apart from its competitors. No matter how complex a customer's design Amtico prides itself on being

Cheers all round

Feeling thirsty? Then providing it goes in a glass, you can be assured of a wonderful selection to choose from at Bablake Wines. Run by the Wyles' family, their range of drinks is truly comprehensive covering everything from wines and spirits, beers and ciders through to mixers and soft drinks, not only from the UK and continental Europe but most distant parts of the world.

The Wyles' family has been contributing to the life of Coventry for many generations. The father of the founder of Bablake Wines, Alderman Vincent Wyles, was in business as a butcher and served as Chairman of the Coventry Meat Traders' Association and subsequently as President of the National Federation of Meat Traders. He was a Conservative member of Coventry Council and received the Freedom of the City in 1897. He was Mayor of the City 1931-32 and his name will always be associated with the building of Trinity Street, a project of which he was the sponsor and which he opened in 1937.

Above: Father of the company founder, Alderman Vincent Wyles. Below: The Coventry Head Offices of Bablake Wines.

For its construction several very old Coventry streets were demolished, including, ironically, Butcher Row and Little Butcher Row! Today it is one of the city's central thoroughfares.

Originally called Bablake Wine Lodge, the company was established in 1929 by Ronald Vincent Wyles at 162 Spon Street, Coventry, where he opened a retail wine merchants in the then 'closed shop' climate of the established wine trade. The fortunes of the firm really took off in the 1950s, and they moved to bigger premises in Harnell Lane, when Vincent, as he was most often known, started wholesaling in a serious way. Six years later the Stoney Stanton Road site was acquired. Vincent's two sons, Martin and Rupert, as well as his son-in-law, David Perry, joined the company and in 1977 the firm moved to its present Kingfield Road site.

It has been a story of continuing success. In the early days they used to ship in their own wines, sherries and ports and bottle and label them themselves. Long gone labels such as Emva Cream, VP Sherries, Spanish Sauternes and Beaudesert were all well known names to Coventry people. Now they have a large bonded

warehouse and their own graphics and design centre and offer hotels, restaurants and pubs a very wide product range, backed up by a first class customer service.

The company weathered the difficult times during the second world war, and when the Retail Price Maintenance was abolished, but they have had their share of good times as well. Since the end of the war prosperity has increased and there has been a marked increase in the demand for wine, which has continued to grow since the 1950s. However, they were not the only ones to see the sales potential of this, the big supermarket chains were also eager to profit from it and started to get into the market for home wine and spirit sales. This pressure was felt so keenly that Bablake eventually pulled out of the retail shops side of operations altogether.

The latest venture in Bablake's history is its new-look cash-and-carry 'off-licence' aimed at the trade and general public alike. A wine-cellar and taproom has been created at their wine, beer and spirits warehouse. It provides an informal atmosphere where customers can browse and ask advice from the trained staff. The company has built up its trade in Coventry and the

Midlands over the years and has established further warehouses in Gloucester and Bristol, providing a focus for expansion into new geographical areas.

The present Board of Directors is made up largely of family members. Martin, the founder's elder son is Managing Director; Rupert, the younger son is Distribution Director, Vivienne (Wiz) Perry, Vincent's youngest daughter is Director and Company Secretary, whilst David Perry, Vivienne's husband is Group Sales Director

Bablake Wines are now one of the leading independent wine and spirit wholesalers in the UK, and though the company's achievements to date are indisputably great, they are not complacent. Plans for the future include the setting up of full e-commerce facilities, and steady ongoing expansion. In short they are looking forward to new challenges in the 21st century and will continue to make good their claim that 'if it's wet and goes in a glass, then Bablake can supply it'.

Above: *Sales Director David Perry on Beaujolais Nouveau day presenting an English 'New Release' to the Jaguar dealership in Dijon, France.*

Going with style

It is said that there are only two certainties in life - death and taxes. Sooner or later everyone will need to call on the services of a funeral director, and fortunately the citizens of Coventry can call on the very best when they need help most.

The well known local funeral directing firm of Grimmett and Timms was founded in 1934 by John 'Jack' Grimmett and Kenneth Timms. Before setting up their own firm, Jack had been involved in running a taxi and wedding car hire business, whilst Ken had been a carpenter. The match was a perfect one and the new business was established as a combined funeral directors and taxi hire firm in Mowbray Street, Stoke.

In the early days the firm used a single motor hearse and following cars; the premises were scented by hot tar used to seal the joints of coffins and the smell of fresh sawdust permeated the air from new coffins, in those days made from solid oak and elm timber on the premises.

Three generations of the family would eventually be involved in the business including Jack's brother Arthur, as well as his wife Eileen and their son Gordon who joined the firm in 1949. In later years Gordon's wife Muriel and eventually their son Graham would work in the business too.

In the early days Jack managed the business and conducted funerals, brother Arthur drove vehicles, Ken Timms made the coffins whilst Eileen managed the firm's finances. In later times when Gordon had joined the business his wife Muriel would do the office work and arrange

Above: *Company founder, Jack Grimmett.*
Right: *Gordon Grimmett.*
Below: *The premises in 1966, with the hearse and limousines outside, Gordon is pictured next to the first car.*

funerals whilst, later still, their son Graham would manage the administration and ultimately conduct funerals himself.

The firm stayed at its first premises for just five years before moving to 118 Albany Road, Earlsdon in 1939.

Edna Dudson who would become the firm's longest serving member of staff contacted Jack Grimmett when she lost her sister in the Coventry Blitz in November 1940. Soon afterwards she began working for the firm on a temporary basis and never left. By the 1990s, then in her eighties and still working, she claimed to have become the longest serving temp in Coventry.

Jack Grimmett died in 1952; his wife Eileen died in 1982. Sadly their son Gordon would die in the same year whilst on holiday in Tenerife. Despite the tragedy of losing her husband Muriel was determined to carry on and took over the management of the firm.

Fortunately when Muriel took over the running of the business in 1982, becoming in the process Coventry's only female funeral director, she had the help of Edna Dudson who by then had already worked for the firm for more than 40 years. The premises were altered and refurbished in 1983. Muriel went on to have the honour of becoming the first woman President of the old established Coventry Guild of Funeral Directors. Later she was elected as President of the Midland Area Federation of Funeral Directors. Under her management Grimmett and Timms became even more well known and respected in Coventry and surrounding areas. In 1996 the company was

acquired by SCI (UK) Ltd but Muriel continued to be a part of the firm's continued success.

Subsequently the premises were again completely refurbished and with added Chapels of Rest. Up-to-date preparation rooms, extra garage space and beautiful, comfortable and welcoming reception areas. A new fleet of Volvo vehicles added to the dignity of the services offered.

Today hearses, limousines, coffins and caskets, a chapel of rest, embalming equipment and Grimmett & Timms unrivalled expertise are all part of a continuing tradition of quality service which incorporates complete arrangements for funeral services and providing a professional, caring and dignified service to the deceased and the bereaved.

We may escape paying our taxes but ultimately we can never escape death. At least when that time comes we can be assured that in Coventry we can have the kind of send-off we would wish for - the firm of Grimmett & Timms intends to continue into the future supplying the same traditional, respectful services that the firm has always been known for.

Top left: A company brochure.
Right: Muriel Grimmett.
Below: The comfortable reception area at the firm's premises.

Lionising achievers, reaching for the stars

Bablake School was built on a piece of land given in 1344 by Queen Isabella, widow of Edward II, called 'Babbelak' for the purpose of building a chapel so that masses may be sung for her; this chapel was a tiny forerunner of St John's or Bablake Church. The old school building itself can be confidently traced back to 1560 when it was recorded that there were 41 children, their overseer, the schoolmaster and two women to keep them, connected with the establishment.

The school was placed on a firm financial footing in 1563 when Thomas Wheatley made the proceeds of a charitable foundation available to the school, the purpose of which was to give free board, clothing and education usually for just two years to poor boys who would then go on to take up apprenticeships locally or further afield.

Thomas Wheatley has been called Coventry's Dick Whittington, coming to the city as a 'poor boy in a white coat' and ending up as its Mayor. He gained his fortune in a remarkable way. He sent his agent to Spain to buy Toledo steel but on inspection the chests which came into his possession were found to contain silver ingots and cochineal. Wheatley attempted to trace the rightful owner of the treasure, but in vain. He determined, therefore, to dedicate the windfall to charitable purposes, and Bablake

Above: *Bablake School Band, 1887.*
Below: *The entire school pictured in 1868.*

School was a beneficiary. Over the years many others were pleased to follow Wheatley's example.

At the end of the 19th century, Bablake absorbed three neighbouring schools known locally as the Gift Schools and moved to its present 11-acre site in 1890. The School grew rapidly in numbers between 1911 and 1936 and during this time it developed into a Grammar School. Fifty acres were bought by the School at Hollyfast Road.

The Second World War presented many problems. The School was not allowed to open until air raid trenches were complete, so a tutorial system came into being. The brand new library was destroyed by bombing in November 1940 and the shelters were also hit. The School was requisitioned as a hostel for building labourers and the decision was taken to evacuate Bablake to Lincoln, where it stayed until the summer of 1943.

The return to Coventry marked the end of the boarding system. After the withdrawal of the Direct Grant System in 1945, the School became Independent until the Direct grant funding was restored in 1957.

The period 1962 to 1977 was a time of great change when there was a great deal of new building undertaken and a major change of ethos was brought about, creating a more liberal and relaxed atmosphere. This was aided by the admission of girls in 1975 when the School became

fully co-educational. 1975 also saw the School amalgamate with King Henry VIII School under the management of the Coventry School Foundation.

The School aims to promote academic excellence by means of a broad, balanced education and to develop the skills, attitudes and knowledge that will enable pupils to adapt to a fast-changing world and to meet the demands of the 21st century, and provide a happy, caring and stimulating well-ordered environment in which individuals may fulfil their potential socially, personally, spiritually and intellectually. Each pupil is encouraged to develop as an individual, is valued in his or her own right, and is encouraged to contribute in his or her own way to the school community. Pupils are encouraged to participate in sporting and cultural activities, to work hard in all they attempt and to achieve the highest possible individual standards.

In 1997, the governors of the Coventry School Foundation, which manages Bablake School, took the decision to improve the facilities of the school by building accommodation for the English, Music and Drama departments. Work started in March 1999 and the Foundation Stone was laid by one of the School's eminent former pupils, Sir John Egan (ex-Managing Director of Jaguar Cars). The £2 million building was finished in July 2000 and everyone is very impressed with it. It will certainly enhance the education offered in these areas.

Top: First Bablake girls, 1975.
Above left: The main entrance of the school.
Below: The English, Drama and Music block.

Steely-eyed and structurally strong

buildings were made using materials recycled from other buildings. The premises didn't look particularly good, but it was adequate for them to fabricate structures for clients.

In 1964 land, again at Torrington Avenue, was obtained from Coventry Corporation. A road to the land was built and a purpose-made building was erected in 1964. The company still occupies the now much extended premises.

Torrington Avenue was the ideal site location to implement the company's strategy of obtaining work direct for industry rather than the usual pattern of obtaining work as subcontractors from the volatile high risk construction industry. The principals of the company were aware of the quantity of steelwork a large production plant

Тhe steel industry is now a mere shadow of what it was, even a couple of decades ago, and many famous names in the business are now simply memories. To survive in this tough economic atmosphere, a company needs to be tough and flexible enough to offer products and service which meet customer demands. Such a company is Coventry based Cov-Con Steelwork, which weathered the fierce economic storms of the late 1980s when 55 per cent of the steel industry went into receivership and many long established firms disappeared forever. In fact they went throughout that period with a full work-force. Doing so strengthened them and the company now is in a good position both in this country and abroad and boasts numerous prestigious contracts with nationally and internationally known companies.

The company was officially formed in 1960 by Neville Aldersley, a newly-qualified Chartered Engineer and Jack Wilkinson, a complete all-rounder in the erection and fabrication of structural steel. They started out renting a plot of land behind a toolmaking company in Torrington Avenue, Coventry.
They obtained only temporary planning permission and their

Top left: *Brian outside the old factory at the rear of Leymols.*
Above right: *Inside the original workshop.*
Right: *Building the Massey Ferguson tractor plant, 1966.*

In the 1960s they had contact with American steel building companies and started to travel extensively in the UK and Ireland erecting their buildings and products. They undertook the erection of the US Navy at Holyloch Nuclear Submarine Base. They were on site for 23 days- it rained for 19! Nowadays they travel much further afield; the firm's work can be seen in Mexico City, Rio de Janeiro as well as throughout Western Europe. All these contracts have one thing in common, they are all won in the face of stiff competition.

Generally the company has had a loyal workforce and when redundancy threatened in 1990 it was to be on a 'last in, first out' basis; the employee with the shortest service had been with the company for 9 years. Fortunately, however, redundancies were not required.

The firm now has four members of the next generation on its books, two Aldersleys and two Wilkinsons. They are continuing the tradition of hard work and excellence established by the founders, who have developed the firm into a leader in its chosen sphere. The company has always invested in the latest technologies and has demonstrated commitment to the highest operational standards so that they are now second to none in terms of quality, efficiency and expertise. They presently offer a state-of-the-art 3D CAD Studio and Structural and Architectural fabrication facilities under one roof so that all elements of a contract can be manufactured in one location.

needs and absorbs. In the Coventry area almost all the needs were provided by companies from the Black Country 30 to 40 miles away.

Torrington Avenue had Standard Triumph at one end of the street and Peugeot (now) at the other. The Massey Ferguson Tractor Plant was less than a mile away and Jaguar, Peugeot, Dunlop, Morris Engines, GEC, Courtaulds, Wickmans, Alfred Herbert and Rolls Royce all 15 minutes away. In the flow production plants when steelwork was wanted, it was wanted now. The geographical advantages gave the company the edge in price and particularly performance. It also changed the lifestyle of its employees. Work in these plants generally required out of plant production hours, which meant weekend working, seven days became everyone's norm. This work was carried out for blue-chip companies and became the lifeblood of the company and saw it through the boom and bust cycles intact.

Top left: *A bridge for Courtaulds.*
Above left: *A typical site under construction (duration three weeks).*
Right: *The entrance to Courts Furniture in Birmingham.*

Insuring risk, ensuring continuity

What started out as a part-time job has grown into a successful insurance business and has provided employment for two generations of the Flanagan family so far.

Patrick Flanagan was working as a part-time insurance salesman while he was Schedules Officer for Coventry Transport. He was obviously gifted in this line of business and he achieved recognition of this by winning the Salesman of the Year award in 1969 sponsored by one of the companies he was selling for. This prompted him to think about setting up business on his own to provide a personal and reliable service which customers could trust. Discussing his thoughts with his wife, Kathleen, he found she was fully behind the idea and he was encouraged to start out. This he did in 1970.

His first business premises consisted of one room at, 17 Allesley Old Road, Coventry which was converted into an office. It was very much a family affair with daughter Bridie and son Kevin helping out. In those early days everyone had to be competent at all

necessary tasks; dealing with customers, familiarising themselves with policies, keeping accounts, emptying bins they all took their turn at doing what had to be done. They offered a range of policies from motor and life assurance to pension schemes.

Their aim was to provide a quality service to the man in the street and small businesses. The business began to grow steadily as more and more people came to appreciate the expertise the Flanagans offered coupled with their honesty in their dealings with their clients.

In the 1970s, offices were very different from now and Patrick's office was a very typical one. All systems were manual, requiring hand written entries in folders and correspondence was typed using a traditional typewriter (remember them?). How different from today when the firm uses top specification computers, e-mail and fully computerised systems.

Above: Company founder, Mr P Flanagan.
Below: Mr Flanagan outside the original premises at 17 Allesley Old Road, Coventry.

At times it felt like a big struggle to build up the business while supporting a family but the first five years of trading saw slow but steady growth. An indication of the extent of this is that the original office became far too crowded and more spacious premises were sought. The ideal spot was found at 115 Radford Road, Coventry - a large corner site on a busy road. It was a convenient location for people to get to and six years after moving the insurance business there, the family branched out and opened a travel agency on the premises.

The family has been fortunate to attract and keep good members of staff who have contributed to their success. They are all very experienced in their field and have a thorough knowledge of their products. In the course of time both Bridie and Kevin left to pursue other interests but their sister, Tina came into the firm and took over the reins when their father Patrick retired in 1998.

This 'retirement' however was not an occasion for relaxing and taking things easy. Patrick was ordained as a Deacon in the Catholic Church and now is occupied serving the community by officiating at weddings, christenings and funerals. He is also involved with work in a number of local schools.

Tina Veasey is continuing the business her father started and intends to build on the success of the business so far by continuing to grow at a steady rate. The Flanagan reputation has been won by giving good service and this will remain a corner-stone of the firm's way of working. The people of Coventry will be able to rely on Flanagan know-how for many years to come.

> *In the 1970s all systems were manual, entries were hand written and correspondence was typed using a typewriter*

Above: *Staff line-up outside the office at the start of the new millennium.*

Chrome plated enterprise

Norman Hay was born in London in 1910 and educated at the London School of Economics. The huge company, which now bears his name, had very humble beginnings in a converted house and workshop in Putney.

Norman Leslie Stephen Hay's association with Coventry began during the second world war. During those years Norman and his wife Joan accommodated evacuated children from Coventry at their home in the countryside and that first link with the city during the 1940s is recalled today with the head office of Norman Hay plc being located in the heart of Coventry.

At the time that Norman and his wife were giving a home to Coventry's young evacuees he was the managing director of a joint venture company with BSA (Birmingham Small Arms) located in Studley, Warwickshire which traded under the name of Monochrome.

Monochrome specialised in plating technology, especially 'hard chrome plating' a process which Norman Hay had pioneered.

During the war Norman worked closely with many famous names in the industry to bring engineering solutions to the war effort. Applications of hard chrome to the rockers on the Rolls Royce Merlin engines of Spitfire fame would massively increase their service life.

Together with George Dowty, Norman also worked to develop a hard chrome plating technique for the split forks on the landing gear of Lysander aircraft, and on the application of hard chrome blades for the revolutionary jet engine so famously designed by Sir Frank Whittle, one of Coventry's most celebrated engineers.

Top left: *Company founder, Mr Norman Hay.*
Above right: *An old Montgomery Plating Co leaflet.*
Below: *Montgomery staff taking a break in the sunshine, circa 1950.*

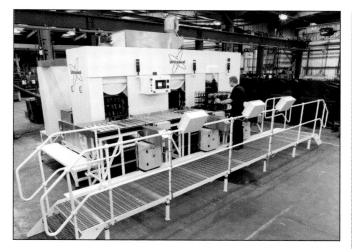

supplier in the development and application of fluorocarbon and fluoropolymer surface coatings; it also offers electroless nickel, anodising and dry film lubricant coating.

BK Engineering, another Norman Hay company, is based at Leighton Buzzard. The company is the precision machining and sheet metal fabrication division of the group offering high quality precision components servicing to a wide range of industries.

Plasticraft in Cannock designs, manufactures, installs and project manages all aspects of immersion process plant, including metal finishing plant, effluent treatment plant and fume exhaust systems.

In Slough yet another Norman Hay company, Ultraseal, uses vacuum impregnation technology to clean and seal a wide range of porous substrates and components. Other applications include ultrasonic cleaning, aqueous cleaning, pressure testing and chromate conversion.

With a Coventry base as well Ultraseal is also internationally famous for supplying solutions to the problems of porous castings and providing equipment and sealant across the globe. Ultraseal International even has a joint venture in India (Ultraseal India) and a subsidiary in the USA (Ultraseal America Inc.).

Surfacetech is another Coventry based company in the group. Surfacetech is a business which provides a range of services including zinc plating, electroless nickel, niflor, silver, alocrom and phosphate conversion for a wide range of industries such as aerospace, automotive, defence and electronics.

Company founder Norman Hay died in 1979: and his lasting legacy is a world famous business supplying the global market with engineering excellence.

After the war those first tenuous links with Coventry were broken as Norman Hay developed his post war business in specialist plating near Heathrow, London's growing main airport. That new company was founded in 1946 and not unnaturally was named Norman Hay Ltd: in the following decades the firm would eventually grow to be very large indeed.

The return to Coventry for Norman Hay Ltd came in August 1988 with the purchase of Montgomery Plating, a long established Coventry company which had grown out of people drawn together at the Rootes Group Aircraft factory during World War II.

Montgomery Plating had grown from very small premises on the outskirts of Coventry to eventually occupy a 32,000 sq ft factory near the city centre in Godiva Place, conveniently situated alongside the city ring road; those premises are now home to Norman Hay plc.

Upon acquiring Montgomery Plating the Norman Hay company invested £5 million in a total site refurbishment, much of the equipment being supplied by a company within the Norman Hay Group, Plasticraft, located at Cannock, Staffordshire.

By the turn of the century the whole Norman Hay group of companies would be controlled from the Norman Hay plc headquarters in Coventry.

Within the group Armourcote is a company based in East Kilbride and Leeds. Armourcote is a leading

Above left, both pictures: *One of the latest machines that the firm has made.*
Below: *The new Ultraseal premises.*

Hard cover for fragile bikers

G F Bennett and Co. Ltd, the 'official' name of Bennetts Insurance Specialists, was established in 1930.

Frederick Bennett had already been involved in selling all kinds of personal insurance and began his new business as a one man insurance broker from the front room of his family home in Coventry.

In 1947 despite petrol rationing meaning few private vehicles on the road, the founder's son joined him in business after serving in the RAF. It was in that year that the firm moved to its first permanent office premises.

The business has been at its present city centre office in Ironmonger Row since 1969 where the firm would become one of the first in the city to provide computer quotations. Today's MD, Michael Bennett, the third generation of his family in the firm joined the business in 1970.

In 1982 Bennetts expanded to provide a nation-wide motorcycle insurance service. That expansion would lead to the opening of a purpose built call centre in 1984 before moving to occupy the current eight storey office building, St George's House in Corporation Street, in 1994.

Sister company Dial Direct was then launched in 1995 to run alongside Bennetts as a direct arm of the business, dealing predominantly with car insurance, before branching out to home insurance.

The greatest challenge for the firm has simply been managing its expansion from modest beginnings to a group which, by the millennium, would have over 600 staff and more than a quarter of a million policyholders.

Today the firm's advanced computerised operation enables it to offer a huge range of insurance schemes many of which are exclusive to Bennetts. They now offer a number of ways to finance premiums for up to 12 months.

Car and home insurance are a major part of the business. However, the firm specialises in motorcycle insurance and was the first insurer to offer an on-line quote through to purchase facility at www.bennetts.co.uk.

Customers living in Coventry can still benefit from the staff's local knowledge and expertise at the Ironmonger Row branch.

From small beginnings Bennetts has become one of the largest insurance intermediaries for bike insurance in the country.

Things have changed an awful lot since Frederick Bennett first sold insurance policies from his front room.

Above: *The front of the Ironmonger Row offices.*
Below: *Michael Bennett and staff outside the Ironmonger Row branch.*

Moving gracefully across the centuries

The dark red and gold vans of the W Grace removal fleet are a well-known sight on the streets of Coventry. They carry the furniture of local families to new addresses and it is the intention of W Grace that moving house which is generally thought of as being a stressful experience goes as smoothly as possible.

It was in 1930 that William Grace who had worked as a coach builder set up in business. He was 23 at the time and he sold his much-loved motor cycle and invested in a 1926 one-ton van and started moving pianos and furniture for local shops. In those days almost every family had a piano in the front parlour. The fact that many of those parlours could only be reached up two or three flights of narrow stairs often created problems for removal men. So William Grace bought a special set of tackle which enabled him to haul pianos up the outside of buildings and in through a window.

For part of the second world war his removal vans were requisitioned for use as ARP ambulances and delivery trucks. After the war William Grace found himself with a rapidly expanding business moving professional firms to new offices and families to new houses. He was helped by his brother Reg and his wife, Nell.

On his retirement in 1973 the business was bought by Bill and Bob Turrall who owned the Leicester Garage in Leicester Causeway. The two brothers always insured that the previous high standards were maintained, adding new ideas and continuing very high labour standards. Paul Garner acquired the business in 1982 and continues to run the company with his father Harry and daughter Nicky from their new premises on the Bilton industrial estate. Here they offer storage facilities in a heated warehouse as well as expertise in moving difficult or valuable items and they still move pianos gracefully!

Above: One of the early lorries at Leicester Causeway. Below: A W.Grace vehicle of 2001. Bottom: The Springfield Road fleet of removal lorries.

Its better to be with a TLC

An Englishman's home, as we all know, is his castle; it is also, in most cases, the largest investment he makes during his lifetime; and more often than not it is bought with a mortgage. Today, thanks to the wide range of advice and services offered by building societies such as the Coventry, it is relatively easy to become a house owner. During the industrial revolution, however, acquiring decent housing posed a problem for the workers who had left their traditional homes in farming communities to come and work in towns and cities. There was no state provision for housing; some employers were able to offer living accommodation and industrial benefactors such as Cadburys who provided model housing estates were assured of a queue of applicants for jobs and a loyal long-serving workforce. Overall, however, there was a serious lack of suitable accommodation for workers and their families. Friendly Societies already existed, providing a range of benefits to subscribing members, and in response to the need for housing a new form of Friendly Society was created; the building society. Members clubbed together and paid monthly subscriptions, and as funds became available the societies bought land; when building commenced, members carried out as much work themselves as their combined skills and time permitted. As each house was completed, a ballot of members was held and the winner moved into the house; however, everybody carried on paying their monthly subscription until all the members had been housed, and not until then would home ownership be transferred from the society to individual members. Finally, any remaining funds were shared out and the society, having fulfilled its purpose, would close.

The first recorded Building Society was formed in Birmingham in 1775. Practices and procedures were modified and refined over the years; the ballot system, for instance, was abolished by the Building Societies Act of 1894. During the 19th century societies began to accept investments from members seeing financial return on their money rather than home ownership, and 'permanent' building societies, offering home loans and saving facilities, became established.

The Coventry Permanent Economic Building Society was founded in February 1884 by a small group of citizens, one of whom was Thomas Mason Daffern, a man of exceptional gifts who became the Society's first secretary, and to whom the Society is indebted for the high standards of integrity and independence which he exercised in his involvement with its affairs over a period of almost half a century. Thomas

Top left: *Thomas Mason Daffern, the Society's founder and first Secretary.*
Left: *The High Street Office pictured in 1934.*

Daffern and his associates gathered in the Coventry Institute and contributed anything from a tanner (6d or 2.5p) to half a crown (2/6d or 12.5p) each, raising a fund totalling £1 2s 6d at a time when Coventry's economy was stagnating due to the decline of the city's traditional industries of silk weaving and watch-making.

Coventry citizens have a long tradition of bravery in the face of economic challenges. The courageous stand taken by these founder members, and the concern with which the Coventry Building Society has continued to protect the financial interests of its members, parallels Lady Godiva's courage in fulfilling her part of a bargain. Her husband, Earl Leofric had agreed to waive additional taxes on his wife's fellow citizens if she rode naked through Coventry. It is in recognition of this that in the early 1970s the Society adopted its famous 'Lady Godiva' logo.

New industries came to Coventry in the late 19th century. Coventry-built bicycles enabled young men and women to enjoy unprecedented independence through the new vogue for cycling; and the developing motor industry, too, chose Coventry as its home. The electrical and chemical industries followed and workers arrived in search of jobs. In the forty years up to 1911 the city's population doubled, creating a greatly increased demand for housing and mortgages; and as workers prospered, they had money

Top: *The original Sir William Reid Dick statue of Lady Godiva, adopted as the Society's symbol.*
Left: *An early advertising campaign.*

to invest. By the beginning of the first world war, the 'Economic', as it was known, had become the largest society in the area in terms of assets, and many local families had begun an association with the Society as investors and borrowers which subsequent generations have been happy to preserve to this day.

A series of mergers in the 1970s and 80s greatly enhanced the Society's assets, and in 1983, following a merger with the Coventry Provident, it was renamed Coventry Building Society.

For well over a century Coventry Building Society has been helping people achieve their dreams of becoming home owners. The many social and economic changes which have taken place during that period have resulted in building societies taking on a significantly different role from that of the early friendly and terminating societies. The legislation governing financial institutions, too, has undergone radical revision. However, Coventry Building Society, led by a dedicated team of financial experts including Chief Executive Martin H Ritchley, who joined the Society in 1970 as Chief Accountant (having previously worked for the Society's auditors), ensures that the Society continues to serve its members in the best and most appropriate way.

Branches have always been a key part of the Society's customer service provision

and at a time when many banks in the UK are reducing their presence on the high street, the Coventry has maintained its investment in its branch network, predominantly based in the Midlands. The Society constantly reviews the branch distribution network, making investment where business opportunities are good and it is cost effective to do so. The Society currently has 50 branch offices.

As new forms of distribution develop, it is essential that the Society offers members a wider choice of convenient access to its services. Recently the Coventry has invested significantly in two internet sites, www.coventrybuildingsociety.co.uk and the specialist website for remortgage business, www.remortgages.co.uk. The early business results from these sites are very encouraging and they intend to develop web-based services still further.

The Coventry has also continued to build on its highly successful telephone operation. The customer service centre, supported by the latest technology, now handles over 800,000 calls each year and is the Society's fastest growing channel of distribution.

Left: An illustration depicting the diversity of Coventry's trade and industry.
Below: The 18th annual Coventry Fun Run, 2000 which was organised and supported as part of Coventry Building Society's community programme.

Foundation by supporting other worthwhile causes and which aims to involve many of the staff in various fund-raising and support activities.

Currently the fifth largest building society in the UK, with assets of over £6 billion, the Coventry Building Society is regularly featured in the national press 'Best Buy' tables for mortgage and savings products. The Society is proud of its building society status which means there are no dividends to pay to outside shareholders. It is efficient and cost effective, with a strong capital base that allows the Society to compete aggressively for new business, whilst ensuring existing customers continue to obtain excellent products and services, reinforcing the Society's reputation, proudly built up over the years. The Society intends to remain true to its slogan, 'TLC not PLC', to prosper and grow in the coming years, and to remain a fine example of a modern building society.

Coventry Building Society is firmly committed to building and maintaining close links with the communities it serves, focusing on community involvement in its heartland, helping a wide range of people and organisations.

In 1998 the Coventry Building Society Charitable Foundation was launched which, to date, has distributed over £180,000 to a wide variety of registered charities within the region. In addition, the Society has recently developed a new community policy which complements the work of the Charitable

Top: *The Society's new headquarters at Binley Park.*
Above left: *A group of beneficiaries receiving grants on behalf of the Coventry Building Society Charitable Foundation.*

*Crowds turn out to enjoy the
Lady Godiva Pageant in 1951.*

Acknowledgments

*The publishers would like to thank
Andrew Mealey, Heritage Services Librarian, for his help in the course of research
and proof-reading, Coventry City Libraries*

*Thanks are also due to
John Thornton who penned the editorial text
and Judith Dennis and Steve Ainsworth for their copywriting skills*